Enter the Kingdom

Enter the Kingdom

Embracing Christian Virtue

Kenneth Swanson

WIPF & STOCK · Eugene, Oregon

ENTER THE KINGDOM
Embracing Christian Virtue

Copyright © 2024 Kenneth Swanson. All rights reserved. Except for brief quotations in critical publications or reviews, no part of this book may be reproduced in any manner without prior written permission from the publisher. Write: Permissions, Wipf and Stock Publishers, 199 W. 8th Ave., Suite 3, Eugene, OR 97401.

Wipf & Stock
An Imprint of Wipf and Stock Publishers
199 W. 8th Ave., Suite 3
Eugene, OR 97401

www.wipfandstock.com

PAPERBACK ISBN: 979-8-3852-2050-2
HARDCOVER ISBN: 979-8-3852-2051-9
EBOOK ISBN: 979-8-3852-2052-6

VERSION NUMBER 06/19/24

Scripture quotations are taken from the New Revised Standard Version Bible, copyright © 1989, Division of Christian Education of the National Council of the Churches of Christ in the United States of America. Used by permission. All rights reserved.

Contents

A Note to the Reader | vii

Introduction: Understanding Virtue | 1

Chapter 1: Humility | 16

Chapter 2: Faith | 27

Chapter 3: Hope | 39

Chapter 4: Agape | 48

Chapter 5: Apatheia | 60

Chapter 6: Peace | 69

Chapter 7: Kindness | 79

Chapter 8: Generosity | 87

Chapter 9: Purity of Heart | 99

Chapter 10: Praos | 106

Chapter 11: Patience | 113

Chapter 12: Wisdom | 120

Chapter 13: The Way Home | 129

Addendum: A Prayer Discipline for Embracing Virtue | 147

Bibliography | 161

A Note to the Reader

ALL THE PERSONAL STORIES told in this book are true. However, most of them have been changed in order to keep confidential the identity of those involved. If I provide the full names of people, I am telling the story exactly the way I remember it happening, or as I remember it told to me by others. If names are not given, or if only first names are used, I have at times changed names, circumstances, details, and in some cases even gender so that the identity of those depicted may be protected. In some instances, I have woven elements of two or more stories into one.

The lists of virtues in the Bible are voluminous. I have chosen twelve virtues for this book. Each of the twelve has a deep grounding in Scripture and Christian tradition. Several of these have such a rich and nuanced meaning in the original Greek of the New Testament and the desert fathers; they cannot be adequately translated into English. Consequently, for some I have kept their Greek names.

I was in parish ministry for nearly fifty years. My parishes have included professional academicians as well as many who could care less about intellectual pursuits. But all desired to grow in faith. When I presented classes in the parish, I always strived to weave scholarly rigor with meaningful narrative. My hope was to cast a net wide enough to be both intellectually challenging and spiritually moving. I believe this was a sound strategy in setting the ground for everyone to grow in faith. This book attempts to follow the same pattern. I want to thank David Swanson for his skilled editorial work on this book. It is massively stronger than it would have been without his insights and suggestions.

Introduction

Understanding Virtue

> *And finally beloved, whatever is true, whatever is honorable, whatever is just, whatever is pure, whatever is pleasing, whatever is commendable, if there is any excellence and there is anything worthy of praise, think about these things.* (Phil 4:8)

WHAT CONSTITUTES MORAL BEHAVIOR? Whether you are religious or secular, there is very little agreement. Most people would define morality as the ability to know and do what is right and good. That may satisfy some, but it immediately begs a slew of other questions: What is right and good? Who defines those things? If we disagree about what they are, does that mean moral behavior cannot be universal? Must morality be particular, personal, and local?

All we need to do is listen to contemporary public discourse to know how true this is. The "moral" agendas of "red" and "blue" politicians are radically different, sometimes even in direct opposition. Both sides claim the mantle of moral superiority. Is there any ground on which to judge between them? Is Majorie Taylor Greene's vision for America more moral than that of Alexandria Ocazio-Cortez? As Alasdair MacIntyre argues in his seminal work *After Virtue*, many would say there is no way to know.[1] He writes we now live in a society that is intellectually dominated by an irreducible pluralism that allows no moral certainty.

1. MacIntyre, *After Virtue*, 10.

In our time in history there are many, particularly in the academy, who deny there can be any accepted moral truth. In the latter half of the twentieth century existentialists staked out the position that each individual creates his or her own morality. As Jean-Paul Sartre declared, "the first principle of existentialism is that man is nothing else but that which he makes of himself. . . Man first of all exists, encounters himself, surges up in the world—and defines himself afterwards."[2] Consequently Sartre claimed the world we live in is valueless. There is no meaning or goal in life. Our humanity places no limits or form on our existence. Each individual is utterly unique and creates value only through personal choice and action, only through his or her own will.

The radical freedom of existentialism has been countered in the twenty-first century by a determinism that declares there is no such thing as free will. The neurobiologist Robert M. Sapolsky asserts in his book *Determined: A Science of Life without Free Will* that no one can be blamed or praised for any thought or action.[3] The objective observations of science, from atoms to culture, show us that everything, including every human choice, is predetermined by the dual imperatives of biological necessity and psychological experience. If everything in life is determined, there can be no freedom. If there is no freedom, there is no morality. If there is no morality, there is no responsibility.

Although influential at the present in the academy, neither existentialism nor determinism is likely to bear the weight of history. For the history of moral philosophy rests on the affirmation that there is a morality that gives meaning to human identity. When we examine the work of those who have thought deeply about morality, there is agreement that moral behavior is enhanced by virtue. Which, of course, begs still more questions, because virtue itself is not easy to define. There is no clear consensus about the role of virtue relative to other moral concepts, let alone what dispositions should be called virtues, or how certain virtues are to be lived out. There are just too many diverse conceptions of virtue for any consensus. There are different rankings of the importance of particular virtues, and incompatible theories of what actually constitutes virtue itself. This is not for the lack of effort. Historically some of humanity's most profound and subtle minds have offered definitions of virtue and its meaning.

---

2. Sartre, "Existentialism Is a Humanism," 349.
3. Sapolsky, *Determined*, 3.

INTRODUCTION

The Criteria for Virtue

With all that disagreement, it may be surprising to learn that almost all systems of virtue have the same three-part structure:

- First, there is an accepted *good life* to which human beings can aspire. In Greek, this good life is called the *telos*, literally meaning "the end." What constitutes the *telos* or goal of human existence may come from divine revelation, or from an awareness of the elements of a just society, or simply from a discernment of what makes a person happy and content.
- Second, there is a contrast between human beings as-they-happen-to-be and human beings as-they-have-the-potential-to-become. We know what happiness is, but all too frequently we are discontented, dissatisfied, restless, and disappointed. In other words, we are not living the good life.
- Third, it is virtue that enables a person to make the transition from the one state to the other. Conversely, vice or sin is what keeps a person malcontent and mired in malaise.

This structure presupposes certain things about reality: that there is a human *telos*; that human beings have the rational ability to understand not just what happiness and unhappiness are, but also what virtues and vices are; and that human beings have the freedom to act. A philosophy that is grounded in the pursuit of virtue and the prohibition of vice will teach adherents how to move from potential to action. That movement must include first becoming free of sin and vice and then embracing the virtues that will lead to and sustain happiness.

It is in that action, that movement we will realize our true nature, and reach our true end. It calls for a combination of reason and will. Intellect will reveal both our true destiny and how to attain it, and the will to act enables us to achieve it.

No practice, of course, takes place in a social vacuum. Historically, a variety of disciplines have been designed to enable people to realize the socially designated *telos*. And the pursuit of virtue demands community—all moral discipline involves standards of excellence supported by at least some element of society. Putting virtue into practice means both accepting the authority of the community's standards and engaging with other practitioners.

Over the past four thousand years four patterns have emerged, creating disciplines for the pursuit of virtue. One is to comprehend virtue in relationship to the law. Another is to see virtue in terms of excellence in the achievement of certain goals or ends. A third, more modern position, giving a nod to existentialism, is to justify morality based on autonomous personal choices, divorced from any *telos* or community standards. And finally, there is the most common perception, which is to understand virtue as the pursuit of what is morally good. These patterns are not mutually exclusive, and often share many assumptions and components.

Law and Virtue

Throughout antiquity, the understanding of virtue was based on the simple acceptance of a cosmic order that gave structure to all existence, dictating the place of each virtue in a total harmonious scheme of human life. Moral truth was found in conformity to this order. In both Hinduism and Buddhism this cosmic order was called *dharma*. The structure of Chinese morality rests on the thought of Lao Tzu (c. 500 BC), who taught conformity to the *tao*. *Dike* in classical Greek meant the "order of the universe," and *diakos* was the person who respected and did not violate that order. For the Stoics, the divine, cosmic law was universal and had no particularity. To live well was to obey the divine law. Zeno of Citium (c. 334–c. 262 BC) wrote, "The goal of life is living in agreement with nature."[4] The good was not found in pursuit of one's individual desires but in submitting to the cosmic order. The Roman Seneca the Elder (54 BC–39 AD) declared the same in "Letters from a Stoic":

> If you live according to nature, you will never be poor. If you live according to opinion, you will never be rich.[5]

The law was even more significant for the Jews. The Jewish *telos*, or standard for human fulfillment and excellence, was manifested in fidelity to the Mosaic Law (traditionally given by God to Moses c. 1300 BC) through personal and community holiness. The Hebrew word *kadosh*, or "holy," had two basic meanings. Its primary definition was "to be set apart" or "to be separate from." This led to the notion of holiness as being utterly unique. That meant both that there was only one God and they alone were God's

---

4. Diogenes Laertius, *Lives*, 87.
5. Seneca, *Letters*, 65.

chosen people. *Kadosh* also had a secondary meaning: "righteousness." If God was holy, or righteous, God's people Israel must also be holy. Individuals within Israel, as well as the nation as a whole, fulfilled this imperative by submission and obedience to the Law of Moses.

This remains true for much of modern Judaism. One day when I was living in Jerusalem, as I walked toward the Western Wall I was stopped by a young Hasidic man, who asked, "Do you keep Torah?" That was his sole criteria for judging me, and the sole criteria for my being allowed to approach the Wall that morning. Whether I was good or courageous or just was of no significance to him. For him the only thing that mattered was fidelity to the Mosaic Law. This is how many Jews define themselves: one is either observant or not. Of course, this is not an exclusively Jewish trait. In fact it's found among the moralistic and dogmatic in all religions and political movements. Psychologically, legalism is legalism. In that, there is not much difference between a fundamentalist Christian who insists on the inerrancy of Scripture and a doctrinaire Communist who is convinced history is determined by dialectical materialism.

The traditional Western understanding rejects this model. Rather it understands virtue as deeply and intimately connected to human freedom. Virtue is not necessarily contingent upon obedience or fidelity to a legal code. Conformity to law, whether those laws are of divine or secular origin, has often hinged on power and coercion, reward and punishment. Whether the source be Hammurabi or Mao Zedong, obey the law and you will benefit; disobey it and you will suffer. In religion, what is gained and lost may have eternal consequences. Ultimately such compliance does not demand virtue, because virtue is an inner frame of mind or cast of character that will enable one to choose the good and the right when there are no rules or law codes for guidance.

Two individuals, therefore, might behave in exactly the same way under similar circumstances, but only one will be virtuous. Virtue, like sin, is defined not only by the act but by the inner motivation. So, if one is acting in response to coercion, or to gain something, or to avoid punishment, that behavior is not motivated by virtue. But if one chooses freely to be faithful to a law code, that fidelity demands virtue. I know many observant Jews for whom this is true. Their fidelity comes not out of legalism, but from a desire to please God with the mystery of grace-infused will.

Virtue as Excellence

Not everyone would divorce virtue from personal gain. In the fourth century BC, Plato argued that success should be the only goal of action. Power was the entire basis for success. Plato pushed this to its logical conclusion, insisting that the ultimate human *telos* was the use of one's intelligence to dominate, and then to use that domination to satisfy one's desires. So, for Plato, virtue was the power to achieve certain results.

Sixteen hundred years later, in pre-Renaissance Italy, Dante (1265–1321) claimed that something was virtuous if it fulfilled its own nature, and did that for which it was ordained. For example, human speech was virtuous when it conveyed a thought with clarity, and wine was virtuous when it pleased the pallet and warmed the heart. Ultimately, though, this attitude led to a complete divorce of virtue from any sense of moral goodness. Niccolo Machiavelli (1469-1527) echoed Plato, writing that political virtue comprised anything that led to success. The English philosopher Thomas Hobbes (1588-1679) took this to its furthest extreme, declaring in war the two cardinal virtues were force and fraud.

In *Introduction to the Principles of Morals and Legislation*, the English philosopher Jeremy Bentham (1748-1832) shared an interpretation of morality that came to be called utilitarianism. For him the individual—beholden to no social or religious structure, nor to any given end for human existence—was an autonomous moral agent. The only human motivation was attraction to pleasure and aversion to pain. For Bentham, moral good was that which resulted in the greatest pleasure, for the greatest number, with the least pain, a conception that remains potent to this day.

Other intellectual movements in the nineteenth and early twentieth centuries understood virtue as a means to an end. G. F. W. Hegel (1770–831) interpreted history as an unending cycle of thesis encountering antithesis resulting in synthesis. Karl Marx (1818–1883) built on Hegel in his theory of dialectical materialism, with the ultimate goal of a historically inevitable worker's paradise. In the Marxist framework, morality and virtue were determined exclusively by what advanced the revolution of the proletariat. For Marx's followers, in places as diverse as the Soviet Union, China, and Cambodia, that end justified any means, even the wholesale imprisonment and murder of millions of innocent people right across the twentieth century.

An entirely other scheme of morality based on excellence emerged from the work of the sociologist Max Weber (1864–1920). Weber analyzed modern society in ways that attempted to understand the justification of power wielded by bureaucrats in government and managers in business. Later sociologists, such as Erving Goffmann (1922–1982) expanded these role-playing characters to include experts in the social sciences, the aesthete consumer, and the therapist. For all of these "social characters" the goal, the *telos*, was excellence in performing their given tasks. So for them, virtue was what enabled success. So today, if virtue is to be equated with excellence, the most significant moralist in contemporary American society might be someone like Stephen Covey (1932–2012), whose best-selling book of virtues was called *The Seven Habits of Highly Effective People*.

The Emergence of the Autonomous Self

Traditionally, virtue had been grounded in the values and standards of the community, understood through reason. The Roman Catholic Scholasticism of Thomas Aquinas (1225–1274) built morality around the merger of reason and revelation. But another way of seeing virtue emerged from the basic affirmations of the Protestant Reformation. Martin Luther (1483–1546) rejected reason as a means of arriving at ultimate truth—for him, the twin pillars of Reformation authority were *sola scriptura* and *sola fide*. Reason had value for judging, measuring, and sorting, but ultimately *telos* was only to be found in biblical revelation, and only experienced through faith and grace.

For those who advocated these Protestant principles, the power of reason to apprehend moral truth was lost in the fall. After that original sin, human beings became powerless to correct or control their passions and impulses—only through God's grace could one move from sin to virtue. Reason was clinical—assessing facts and patterns—but in the realm of practice, it could speak only of means, not ends. This separation of reason from revelation led to the great schism of religion from science. In the seventeenth century, when Rene Descartes (1596–1660) asserted the ultimate ground of human certainty was found in reason—"I think therefore I am" (*cogito ergo sum*)—he was countered by Blaise Pascal (1623–1662), who declared the only certainty was in faith: "I believe, therefore I am" (*fide ergo sum*). Both assertions had not only teased apart reason and revelation, but moved understanding of truth from the community to the individual: "*I* think, therefore *I am*"; "*I* believe, therefore *I am*."

The seeds of that intellectual shift had been planted by another affirmation that emerged in the Protestant Reformation. In April 1521, when Martin Luther was forced to appear before the Imperial Diet in Worms, the combined weight of religious and secular authority called on him to recant his heresy or face excommunication and burning at the stake. Standing before the electors of the Holy Roman Empire, including Emperor Charles V himself, Luther was unbowed, and is said to have declared to that august body,

> Unless I am convinced by Scripture and plain reason—I do not accept the authority of the popes and councils, for they have contradicted each other—my conscience is captive to the Word of God. I cannot and I will not recant anything for to go against conscience is neither right nor safe. God help me. Amen.[6]

How significant was Luther's insight? It ultimately led to the Enlightenment's elevation of the individual over the community, and reason over revelation (the latter of which Luther would have deplored). When it came to morality, Enlightenment and post-Enlightenment thinkers rejected faith, but in limiting themselves to the realm of reason and observation, they ultimately denied that there was any essential human nature. What, then, was the justification for morality? Was it reason itself? And if not reason, then what?

In the eighteenth and nineteenth centuries great minds such as David Hume, Immanuel Kant, Soren Kierkegaard, and Friedrich Nietzche all tried and failed to establish a universal system of morality. Traditional concepts of virtue seemed to have no place in their world. As stated above, in the twentieth and twenty-first centuries existentialism and determinism made absolutely no claim for universality in morality. Both views asserted that moral judgments could be neither true or false, since there were no rational methods to prove or disprove them. The key questions become: What rules are we to follow? Why should we? In modern society, individuals are free to agree or disagree on what constitutes the good life of humanity. The result of this is that rules and regulations become the primary concept of the moral life, and qualities of character come to be prized only because they lead one to follow the right set of rules. And isn't that simply another form of legalism?

---

6. Quoted in Bainton, *Here I Stand*, 144.

INTRODUCTION

Virtue as the Morally Good

If those multiple ways of understanding virtue make your skin crawl, relax. All across history most intellectuals conceived of an entirely different way of comprehending virtue. In his dialectics Plato (c. 426–c. 324 BC) wrote about the moral vision of his teacher Socrates (died c. 399 BC). Socrates rejected the notion that virtue should be defined by excellence and success by arguing that true virtue was the ability to become morally good, especially when confronted by difficult circumstances. Socrates defined the four "cardinal" virtues as prudence, temperance, fortitude, and justice. In Socrates' scheme, bodily appetites must be restrained by reason; danger must be met by courage. Reason itself could discern truth and beauty through *sophia* or wisdom. Ultimately this would lead to justice. Socrates called these virtues "cardinal"—from the word *cardo*, meaning "hinge"—because he believed that all human destiny would turn on whether people would be able to manifest those qualities.

Aristotle (384–22 BC), the great systematizer, built on the ideas of both Socrates and Plato. The ruling will for Aristotle was the *logos*, or the eternal divine reason, the pursuit of which was the *telos* of human existence. Virtues were those qualities that would enable individuals to attain this state. But the pursuit of those virtues was itself part of the good life, not just the means of attaining it. The exercise of virtue was a choice; it was not an intuitive natural response. One became virtuous through study and training, learning both what the virtues were and how to choose them. The virtuous person knew what she was doing, and why she was doing it.

In this, virtue required judgment: to do the right thing in the right way in the right place at the right time. The law prohibited, while virtue liberated. But only in moderation. For Aristotle, virtue was found in the space between two extremes: courage between rashness and timidity, temperance between prodigality and parsimony, prudence between profligacy and covetousness, justice between anarchy and despotism. But for Aristotle these virtues were not universally accessible and could be fully known only by a highly trained elite. True virtue was a state only known to those highly trained citizens exercising their given roles within the structure of the polis, or city-state.

The Development of Christian Virtue

Early Christian thinkers found themselves caught in a triple tension, reflecting on the meaning of the life and teaching of Jesus in the context of both the Hebrew and the Hellenistic worldviews. The Christian *telos* grew out of Jewish tradition, which taught that humanity was created to live in perfect intimacy and harmony with God, with one another, and with creation itself. Sin destroyed that equilibrium, resulting in alienation, strife, and ultimately death. But in the crucifixion of Jesus, the power of sin was destroyed, and in his resurrection a new path to virtue and salvation was available to all believers.

How does one take the first step down that path to righteousness? Jesus' imperative was fierce and uncompromising. Reflecting on Jewish teaching, he said, "You must be perfect as your Father in heaven is perfect" (Matt 5:48). Since that holy perfection was found in the Law of Moses, Jesus declared, "not one letter, not one stroke of a letter, will pass away from the law . . ." (Matt 5:18). But in the Gospel accounts, Jesus was famously scornful of slavish obedience to the law, and pointed to another way of living, one that rested on freedom. As he taught, "Cure the sick, raise the dead, cleanse the lepers, cast out demons; as you have freely received, freely give" (Matt 10:8).

That dialectic between law and freedom opened up the mystery of Christian sanctification. Believers were called from sin to holiness, and certain freely exercised virtues would nurture that process. In the New Testament, these virtues were usually described as "gifts of the Holy Spirit" (1 Cor 12ff.), the three primary gifts being faith, hope, and love. But St. Paul added wisdom, discernment, knowledge, prophecy, and healing. In his Letter to the Galatians, Paul listed the "fruit of the Spirit" as love, joy, peace, patience, kindness, generosity, faithfulness, gentleness, and self-control, concluding "there is no law against such things" (Gal 5:22–23).

This state of grace could only be fulfilled in community, in what the New Testament referred to as "the body of Christ." In Colossians, Paul gave a description of the virtuous Christian, one seeking to live out the New Testament *telos*:

> As God's chosen ones, holy and beloved, clothe yourselves with compassion, kindness, humility, meekness, and patience. Bear with one another and, if anyone has a complaint against another, forgive each other; just as the Lord has forgiven you, so you also must forgive. Above all, clothe yourselves with love, which binds

everything together in perfect harmony. And let the peace of Christ rule in your hearts, to which indeed you were called in the one body. And be thankful. Let the word of Christ dwell in you richly; teach and admonish one another in all wisdom; and with gratitude in your hearts sing psalms, hymns and spiritual songs to God. And whatever you do in word or deed, do everything in the name of the Lord Jesus, giving thanks to God the Father through him. (Col 3:12–17)

The first Christians to prioritize a personal intimacy with God over communal fellowship in Christ were monks in the Egyptian and Syrian deserts in the fourth century. The greatest of these, St. Anthony (c. 251–c. 356), developed the discipline of Christian virtue in three stages. First, a monk was to practice self-scrutiny and asceticism, enabling him to become fully conscious of himself as God's creature. Secondly, a monk was to withdraw into solitude to face his inner demons, his personal sins, confronting and repenting of them, seeking God's forgiveness. Finally, once in perfect intimacy with God, the monk was to re-enter the community in order to train younger people in the discipline.

Two generations of monks practiced these spiritual disciplines, which were systematized by Evagrius Ponticus (c. 345–99). For Evagrius, there were three stages of spiritual progress: the *pratike* or "practice," which allowed one to become conscious of sin and virtue through repentance and purgation; the *theoria physike*, or true knowledge of all things in creation, which resulted in correct discernment of the truth and moral law in both nature and Scripture; and finally *theoria tes agias triados*, or knowledge of the Trinity, a deep, intimate, contemplative, beatific union with God.

His foremost disciple was John Cassian (c. 360–430), who took Evagrius's work to the Latin-speaking West, where Benedict of Nursia (c. 480–547) wove these concepts into a practice that has dominated Western Christianity since the sixth century. Benedictine spiritual formation maintained Evagrius's three steps of purgation, illumination, and contemplative union. It codified sin and virtue, and distinguished the goal of contemplative prayer—which was intimacy with God—from that of petition and intercession, which were for building Christian community.

Christian Virtue and the Morally Good

From Ambrose and Augustine in the fourth and fifth centuries to Abelard and Aquinas in the twelfth and thirteenth centuries, there was also a stream of Christian thought that looked beyond the more narrow *telos* of intimacy with God, and linked virtue to the broader Hellenistic concepts of the good, the true, and the beautiful. The initial challenge facing Christian thinkers was the relationship between pagan virtues and biblical virtues. Should the pagan virtues be transformed and integrated into the Christian vision, or rejected as the devil's work in order to champion biblical revelation as the all-sufficient guide? Most theologians felt the task was one of integration. Ultimately, Pope Gregory the Great (c. 540–604) decided to list seven virtues, mirroring his list of "seven deadly sins." In addition to Socrates' four "cardinal" virtues of courage, prudence, temperance, and justice, Gregory added the three "theological" virtues of faith, hope, and love.

Following Aristotle, these theologians taught that the pursuit of virtue in itself fulfilled the divine will. This affirmation contributed to a unified medieval vision, an idealized view of reality as an integrated order in which the temporal reflected the eternal. Everything had its place in the overall scheme, a vision shared by medieval Christians (Abelard and Aquinas), Jews (Maimonides) and Muslims (Ibn Raschd). Grace and reason worked in harmony. One could know what was true and false, as well as what was good and evil, by both divine revelation *and* human reason. The medieval Christian vision differed in significant ways from Aristotle, but it retained his basic three-part structure: we know the good; we do not possess the good; but (with grace cooperating with reason) we have the ability to obtain the good. Virtue is what enables us to make that transition.

There Is Another Way

As delineated above, that Christian vision was coopted by a championing of reason and the autonomous self by Enlightenment thinkers and those who followed them over the last three centuries. But in so narrowly parsing human motivation and behavior, in cutting morality off from the affirmations of faith and the consensus of social institutions, post-Enlightenment moral philosophy has become so constricted that its practitioners are talking only to themselves. The fact is, people *do* have a sense of what is right and wrong.

INTRODUCTION

Let's just admit it: we have lost our way into the wilderness. Where do we turn to find a way out of this intellectual morass? No one wants to go back. But if a clock is telling the wrong time, it needs to be reset. When we are lost, we need to go back to that place where we last knew where we were. So—if we've become lost and want to find a way home, a way out—the only intelligent thing to do is go back to the last place where we knew the way.

Where is that?

I would argue that the Christian humanism of Martin Luther stood at that hinge, where the synthesis of Christian theology and classical Hellenistic philosophy gave us a clearly articulated, universally accepted moral vision. In advocating faith and grace over reason, Luther created a new landscape, but he never claimed that they were mutually exclusive. He never imagined a human destiny cut off from either the *telos* of the community or a relationship with God. Luther was not wrong; subsequent moral philosophers simply misplayed his cues. Because there is a way for the free, individual self to naturally bridge the gap between faith and reason. And that bridge can be found in a new understanding of virtue.

The vast majority of people accept the basic three-part structure of traditional moral teaching. First, there is a recognized moral life, which human beings can pursue and achieve. As written above, this *telos* may come from a divine revelation, but it can also come from an innate sense of justice, or from an understanding of what it is that makes a person happy and content. Second, there is a difference between who we are and who we have the potential to be. It doesn't matter if you ask a plumber or a physicist; we know we have unfulfilled moral potential. Third, virtue is what enables a person to move from one state to the other.

Even for a person of faith, much about what is morally good can be discovered within nature and society. In his essay "Right and Wrong as a Clue to the Meaning of the Universe," C. S. Lewis (1898–1963) wrote that when people argue they almost always appeal to an accepted standard of behavior, even when they may disagree on the particulars.[7] In the 1970s Jimmy Carter and Leonid Breshnev had totally different visions of human rights, but they both appealed to some unnamed but accepted standard of what is morally just and right. Lewis argued that this moral standard is the "law of human nature." Unlike natural laws, which simply reflect facts that can be observed (a stone when dropped falls, showing the law of gravity), this moral law is not found in what human beings actually do, but in what

---

7. Lewis, *Mere Christianity*, 3.

they *ought* to do. It is not instinct. It is not social convention. It is often not even what benefits either the individual or the greater good. But we know it. We experience it in the world and recognize that it points beyond the world to something beyond fact, beyond sense perception, beyond reason.

In the thirteenth century Thomas Aquinas championed the addition of the three theological virtues of faith, hope, and love to prudence, temperance, courage, and justice, the four cardinal virtues of pagan tradition.[8] For Aquinas, this gave symmetry to a vision of sin and virtue: the seven deadly sins were matched by seven virtues. It also helped advance his agenda of integrating Aristotelian concepts into Christian theology. In spite of valiant attempts by Roman Catholic apologists to validate this structure, it remains brittle and artificial. So, in the structure of virtue I am proposing, I have jettisoned Socrates' cardinal virtues and replaced them with concepts drawn from biblical revelation.

Like Aquinas, I see the appeal of symmetry and as I have previously written about ten deadly sins, I would like to have ten matching virtues; but that is simply not enough. The New Testament literally lists over thirty virtues. But all can be touched on with a generous twelve. So, to faith, hope, and love I have added nine others, chosen because of the role each has played in the history of Christian spirituality. Some of them are difficult if not impossible to translate into English, so for those I will use their Greek forms as presented in the New Testament or understood by the desert fathers. The nine additional virtues are humility, *praos* (attentive discipline), wisdom, *apatheia* (inner freedom), *upomone* (patient good courage), kindness, peace, generosity, and purity of heart. Many others could have been chosen with both biblical and historical warrant. But to my mind these twelve, in contrast with the ten sins, create a full picture of the Christian *telos*.

These virtues all have a natural dimension and can be experienced by anyone. But each also has a spiritual dimension that can be known only in grace. Many thinkers, from Socrates to Cicero to Spinoza to Emerson, have declared virtue is its own reward. But the spiritual aspect of Christian virtue points beyond a natural state of being in the world. The ultimate goal of Christian virtues is to draw those who practice them into a relationship with God. The *telos* of the Christian life looks beyond virtue, seeing it simply as a means to experience God's love, and be led by that love to participate in a redemptive community. The spiritual virtues are like gates

---

8. Aquinas, *Summa Theologica*, 104.

opening into the Kingdom of God. When we experience the fullness of love, or faith, or hope, we will encounter the reality of God.

As I wrote above, the full expression of spiritual virtue can only be known as a gift of grace. No human being is capable of experiencing the spiritual aspect of these virtues on his or her own. Jeff Bezos is not rich enough to buy faith. Faith is a free gift of grace. Albert Einstein was not brilliant enough to discover hope. Hope is a free gift of grace. Mother Teresa of Calcutta was not righteous enough to experience unconditional love. That too comes to us as a gift of God's grace.

That doesn't mean these virtues are beyond our grasp but only that they can be completely realized only in grace. If the first step of spiritual maturity is to be conscious, being aware is the first step of embracing virtue. The natural aspects of a virtue like faith become a pathway to fully understanding the spiritual aspects of faith.

There are basic assumptions that are foundational to this vision. There is a good life. Human beings can become far more than we are, but sin prevents us from achieving our promise. Virtue enables us to know and embrace the good.

Is there universality in this? Of course; this is not just the Christian or even biblical way of understanding human nature. But in spite of sound insights from contemporary psychology, philosophy, and sociology, sinfulness is still the most helpful way to comprehend who we are as human beings, and why we are unhappy. And virtue is still the context in which to discover abiding contentment.

It may be revelation that tells us sin is rooted in rebellion against God. It may be revelation that tells us that living for God and for others with intimacy and vulnerability is the foundation of happiness and well-being. But the effect of both sin and virtue on happiness is evident. This is a universal observation that holds sway over even the most blatant postmodern subjectivity. If you read through this book and are not filled with a desire for each of the virtues, perhaps you are too locked up in yourself to hear or see that there is another way, a better way, one that will not just lead to a deeper contentment but fulfill your true identity.

Chapter 1
Humility

> *He has told you, O mortal, what is good; and what does the Lord require of you but to do justice, and to love kindness, and to walk humbly with your God?* (Mic 6:8)

> *Let the same mind be in you that was in Christ Jesus,*
> *who, though he was in the form of God,*
> *did not regard equality with God*
> *as something to be exploited,*
> *but emptied himself,*
> *taking the form of a slave,*
> *being born in human likeness.*
> *And being found in human form,*
> *he humbled himself*
> *and became obedient to the point of death—*
> *even death on a cross.* (Phil 2:5–8)

ALL ACROSS HISTORY, PHILOSOPHERS, theologians, and other deep thinkers have declared that happiness, well-being, and purpose are found in the pursuit of virtues. But despite all this most people remain indifferent to the cultivation of the virtuous life. Sometimes this is because the virtue itself seems to lack appeal. For example, the opposite of humility is pride, which some would consider a virtue itself. Yet, just as pride is the parent of all the other sins, humility is the ruling virtue that opens wide the gate into God's kingdom.

HUMILITY

Still, many shy away from humility. What kind of response does the word "humility" evoke in you? Is it positive or negative? Is humility something you instinctively desire or not? Let me put it this way: if I invited you to my house for lunch, and told you for dessert I was serving "a big piece of humble pie," would you want to come? Obviously not. And little wonder. One definition of humility in the *Oxford English Dictionary* is the "quality of having a low opinion of one's self, to be meek and self-denigrating," with a secondary meaning of being "unpretentious." But if humility is "the opposite of pride," and if the self-absorption of pride is the heart of sin and the root of unhappiness, shouldn't the alternative be desirable?

The clear quandary in embracing humility is that we have all been taught that there is nothing virtuous about self-denigration. Just as the notion of pride creates two minds in us—healthy self-esteem as opposed to alienating self-absorption—humility has the same positive and negative aspects. But the virtue of humility is not feeling badly about oneself; that is pusillanimity, which in reality is as self-absorbed as arrogance. If pride is self-absorption, then the virtue of humility manifests as selflessness. The key to humility is to not be conscious of self at all.

We all know what this selflessness feels like. There is the natural humility we experience when we do the things we love. Whether this happens when you draw or dance or garden, there are moments when you become humbled, transparent, lost in the joy of the activity. When we listen to music we love, or are captivated as our favorite player leads a fourth-quarter comeback, or become entranced by the emotional power and visual beauty of a splendid film, we all have moments when we transcend ego and become selfless.

I was once invited to watch a rehearsal of the Joffrey Ballet from backstage at the New York State Theatre in Lincoln Center. The choreographer Gerald Arpino was coaching a young dancer through an intricate solo piece. When she misstepped, Arpino stopped her, and patiently demonstrated what he wanted. After a couple of run-throughs without music, she had it down. Then he wanted to see her dance to the music. With the first note of the lush Romantic melody she became transformed, utterly engaged, giving herself over completely to music and movement. It lasted three, maybe four minutes. Watching her, I was transfixed, but she was transported. When it ended to Arpino's vocal satisfaction, the young dancer breathing heavily, face radiantly flushed—and walked off stage right past me. Sailing by without pausing, she recognized my wonder, our eyes locking for just an instant as she said, "Joy." That is what humility feels like; when we are not conscious of self at all.

The times in my own life when I sometimes achieve this state of transparency and transcendence is when I am preaching and teaching. Once when I was a young priest at Grace Church in New York City, I was scheduled to preach on Palm Sunday. In the days leading up to the service, I was more than a bit anxious; I knew there would be a huge congregation, and I felt I had written a very weak sermon. As the liturgy began, I felt the tentacles of panic reaching for me. I was sure I was going to preach an awful sermon and humiliate myself in front of hundreds of people. But once I stepped into the pulpit, I experienced one of those inexplicable moments of grace. It was as if I became so transparent, God's Word simply flowed through me. As I was greeting people leaving the church after the service, and I was complimented time and again on the powerful sermon, I could only respond with complete honesty: I had nothing to do with it. Certain that I had been the beneficiary of the gift of the Holy Spirit, I went home filled with gratitude. Relaxing later in the afternoon, watching an early-season Yankee game on television, I found myself offering spontaneous prayers of thanksgiving to God, that God had enabled me to experience the depth of humility.

But pride is a stubborn thing, and it never takes long for it to rear its ugly head. Before long thoughts of self-regard crept into my mind. "You know, that was actually a pretty good sermon." And a bit later, "No, it was an outstanding sermon." And before I knew it, "I doubt if there was anyone else in New York who could have preached such a good sermon."

Humility Is the Enemy of Pride

One of humanity's greatest achievements of imagination is *The Lord of the Rings* by J. R. R. Tolkien. In the twenty-first century, because of the spectacular success of Peter Jackson's Oscar-winning movies, almost everyone knows the story. On the surface, it is a children's fantasy, telling the tale of how elves, dwarves, human beings, and hobbits ally themselves as the forces of good, locked in a mortal struggle with evil.

I say that it is children's fantasy on the surface, because the rich complexity and intellectual power behind this book is decidedly mature. Tolkien, the professor of English literature at Oxford for forty years, created entire histories and mythologies as the foundation for the story. This background material was published after his death as *The Silmarillion*, covering thousands of years of Middle Earth's mythology. Purely out of his own imagination he also created an entirely cogent and linguistically sound language spoken by his elves. The introduction to the great saga was published as a separate book called *The Hobbit*.

Yet the real power of *The Lord of the Rings* is buried deep below the surface. Critics and scholars have found metaphors threaded throughout *The Lord of the Rings*. Some felt that it was really the story of the struggle between democracy and fascism that culminated in an allied victory in World War II. Others wrote that Tolkien was intent on creating a mythology for the British people. But I would argue, along with others, that *The Lord of the Rings* is a metaphor for the Christian life. Tolkien was a devout Roman Catholic. He wrote as children's fantasy the story of what it means to be a Christian. It is the story of the struggle between sin and redemption, between humility and pride.

Pride is a fundamental theme in both *The Lord of the Rings* and *The Hobbit*. In the latter, the homebody hobbit Bilbo Baggins is sent from the comfort of his hearth on a mysterious quest. He doesn't know exactly where or why he is going, only that he is being compelled by a force greater than him. His journey takes him through a dark forest called Brethil, at the heart of which is a great spider so malevolent, so evil it draws everything that enters the forest into its web to control, consume, devour. Bilbo is drawn against his will into the Spider's web, where he struggles to free himself, but to no avail. But as soon as Bilbo gives up struggling—at the moment when he realizes he has no strength left, that he is completely broken and is ready to die—a power he had never known suddenly breaks into his heart and mind. This new and wonderful power gives him the strength to break free. That spider is Tolkien's metaphor for pride—sucking everything to it, in order to control, dominate, and destroy.

But Tolkien also shows us the way out of pride. It can never be broken by human effort. We cannot educate our children to grow up free from its grip. The only thing that will free us from pride is to be broken and left empty-handed. Like Bilbo Baggins caught in the spider's web, if we are broken, if we surrender unconditionally, we will discover that there is a power that will draw us into a new quality of life.

The Power of Humility

As I noted earlier, humility is greatly misunderstood. Humility is not groveling. Humility is a state of complete selflessness, the opposite of pride. Only in rejecting prideful self-absorption and accepting humility are we free to serve others and both accept and offer love. That is the true meaning of humility: embracing our own weakness so that we can be drawn into the life of God.

Hudson Taylor (1832–1905), the great British missionary to China, once wrote that all the men and women who accomplished great things in the kingdom of God were conscious of their own weakness. But it is through their weakness that the power of God became manifest in the world. We don't have to look far for the evidence in the biblical narrative. The Bible is full of godly men and women who accomplished God's will. Not because they said, "I can do this." Not because they said, "I am strong" or "I am brilliant" or "I can dominate." No, it was because they said, "I *can't* do it." "I am weak." Who was like this? Abraham, Moses, Gideon, David, Jeremiah, and Mary, the mother of our Lord . . . in weakness they all had faith that God would be with them.

Taylor, who led the China Inland Mission to astonishing success, was himself a manifestation of this kind of humility. Once when he was visiting Britain the leader of the Church of Scotland said to him, "You must sometimes be tempted to be proud because of the wonderful way God has used you. I doubt if any man living has had greater honor." Taylor answered, "On the contrary, I often think that God must have been looking for someone small enough and weak enough for him to use, and that he found me."[1]

When I first met my friend B. J. Weber in 1980, he was involved in a very difficult ministry in and around Times Square in New York City. At first, his normal working hours were from nine at night until five in the morning, and his parish was the streets of Midtown Manhattan. He ministered to the homeless, to runaways, and to those who worked the streets outside the law. During a period when the state of New York emptied its mental hospitals, his "parishioners" grew into the hundreds.

B. J. was very successful in helping people to turn their lives around, and his ministry began to attract media attention. In 1984 he was invited to go to Washington, DC to testify to a United States Senate committee about his ministry with those he called "the poorest of the poor." When

---

1. Taylor, *Hudson Taylor's Spiritual Secret*, 201–2.

the actual day arrived, B. J. described it as the best day of his life. He was flying high. This was the opportunity he had worked so hard to achieve, the breakthrough he'd been hoping would happen for years. In that Senate committee room, for an hour he would be the center of attention of the national media.

That day, just before the committee hearing, he was scheduled to have lunch with three senators: Tom Harkin of Iowa, Scoop Jackson of Washington, and Howard Baker of Tennessee. After he arrived at the Senate dining room, he needed to wash up, so he excused himself to go to the men's room. Standing at the sink, he accidentally spilled water all down the front of his trousers. They were light-colored, so there was no way he could disguise it. Looking down, he felt utterly humiliated. As hard as he tried to figure out how, there was no way to cover it up. As he walked back to the table filled with those powerful men, they stared at him bemusedly. He made a lame comment about spilling water and they all laughed out loud. B. J. was no longer riding high. His pride, his self-absorption, had been broken. When he sat down at the table, he no longer had any desire to draw attention to himself or his ministry. B. J. reflects back on that moment as a great blessing. It set him free in humility to be a selfless advocate for the urban poor and homeless, without a trace of self-aggrandizement.

Tolkien was conscious as well of how humility can unleash power. The four hobbits who were on the quest in *The Lord of the Rings* left the wonderful comfort and security of their lives in the Shire. Without fully realizing why they were doing it, they embarked on a self-sacrificial mission. Only later did they realize Frodo was called to destroy the great Ring of Power. But the foremost embodiment of humility in *The Lord of the Rings* is the human character called Strider. At the beginning of the trilogy, Strider is a Ranger, one of a rough group of men who guard the frontiers of the Shire, preventing any evil from breaking in. Hobbits despise the Rangers, who appear to them to be uncouth, dirty, and uncivilized. Hobbits would never think to invite a Ranger into their own homes, even as the Rangers protected them and secured their well-being.

When Bilbo's nephew Frodo, his friend Sam, and cousins Merry and Pippin continue their quest, Strider accompanies them. They're glad to have him along for protection, even if they don't trust him. Only as the purpose of the journey becomes clearer is it revealed that Strider, the one whom they despise even though they rely on his strength, is in reality the lost king. In the final battle between good and evil, it is Strider who leads the great army of justice and goodness to glorious victory. Strider—thought to be debased, low, and ignoble—is revealed to be King Aragorn. In narrative form, Tolkien uses Strider to describe the meaning of Jesus' saying, "Those who are humble themselves will be exalted" (Matt 23:12). Those who live in humility will know something that the prideful will ever know: the redemptive love of God.

When I think about historical figures who have lived out this kind of humility, one who looms in my consciousness is Eric Liddle. Although he has long been revered in his native Scotland, the greater world only came to know him through the Academy Award–winning movie *Chariots of Fire*. During the early 1920s Liddle was considered not only the fastest man on earth, but also the world's premier rugby player. He was never defeated in international competition and won the gold medal in the four-hundred-meter dash at the Paris Olympics in 1924.

Liddle was also a deeply committed Christian, and very often felt the tug between the values of the world and values of the kingdom of God. He took a degree in theology at New College, Edinburgh, with the goal of becoming a missionary to China. But he continued to run because he believed his speed was a gift of God and brought glory to God. He also felt closest to God while he was running. When criticized by his sister for delaying his work in China in order to train for the Olympics, he responded that he knew it was God's will for him to run because, as he declared, when he did, "I feel God's pleasure."[2]

After the Olympics, he left the world of fame and success, traveling to northern China, where he began to work in obscurity, leading people to faith in Jesus Christ and planting Chinese churches. The world forgot about Eric Liddle. There wasn't much interest in the media over a Scotsman humbly serving the poor in northern China. Early in World War II, Liddle was captured by the Japanese and put in a prison camp. He died there, of typhoid, in total obscurity. The rest of the world didn't know of his death until four years later. He had spent the last twenty years of his life completely cut off from any power, or fame, or riches, but Eric Liddle could have cared less.

The American theologian Langdon Gilkey was with Liddle in the same Japanese prison camp. At a dinner in the late 1990s Gilkey told me that over the course of his life he had only met only one saint. It was Eric Liddle, who was offered the comfort of house arrest by his Japanese captors because of his fame, but refused. He spent his time in the prison camp

---

2. Keller, *King's Cross*, 43.

teaching, preaching, and ministering to the sick. Dozens of young Chinese Christians were mentored by him there. After the war it was these young men and women who spread Christian faith in China. Several research institutions estimate the number of Christians in China grew from one million in 1945 to over one hundred million today. Over the past four decades Christianity in China has grown faster than anywhere else in the world.[3] Those millions, and the millions more who will follow in the future, are Eric Liddle's true legacy.

Humility Gives a True Sense of Self

Humility enables us to see ourselves truthfully, with all of our shortcomings and failures. We can acknowledge our sins and vices, without feeling any necessity to cover them up. The seventeenth-century Anglican divine Jeremy Taylor wrote in *Holy Living* that humility frees us from the need to make a favorable impression on others in the hope they will think we are better than we actually are.[4] Free from what others say or feel about us, we can simply accept ourselves. We are who we are. No need to create a false persona or a false impression.

In the early 1980s when I was working at St. Bartholomew's Church, I organized a group of junior clergy from the five largest Episcopal parishes in Manhattan. We met once a week to discuss issues facing the church and the city. I have never been in a group with more posturing, arrogance, and bravado. Each young priest was out to establish himself or herself as the smartest and most godly person in the room, and certainly as the one most destined for ecclesiastical success. That is, everyone but a young priest from southern Africa. While we all clamored to get a hearing, he remained calmly silent. He only spoke when asked to at the very end of the meetings. After a time, we all began to look forward to what he would say. In a few months, he had become the leading person in the group, and although most wouldn't admit it, we all knew he was the smartest and most godly person in the room. He went back to Africa and I didn't see him again for over thirty years. We met for lunch in Kwa-Zulu Natal, South Africa, in 2007. He had just been elected bishop.

As St. Francis de Sales (1567–1622) wrote in *Introduction to the Devout Life*, humility also enables us to honestly access and embrace our

---

3. Stark and Wang, *Star in the East*, 2–3.
4. Taylor, *Selected Works*, 88.

talents and achievements as gifts of grace. During my first year as rector of Grace Church in Millbrook, New York, I had a well-known and highly accomplished parishioner. Elderly, and wrestling with illness, he was frail but still displayed a lively mind and winsome personality. Over his career he had been managing editor of the *New York Times*, written significant books, traveled the world, held important diplomatic posts, and befriended many famous and powerful people. When I complimented him on the depth and scope of his success, he laughed and said, "There's nothing special about me. I was just an average guy who was in the right place at the right time." And he meant it.

Because a humble person truly knows and accepts herself, she can also honestly evaluate others. The humble among us feel no need to belittle or tear down anyone else. On the contrary, they have the ability to freely praise the talents and good work of others without feeling it diminishes their own self-worth. And true humility enables people, knowing themselves as they truly are, to stand with strength for what they believe is right. In the film *Chariots of Fire* Eric Liddle would not let the world violate his Christian values. In 1924 when he was the overwhelming favorite, he refused to run in the hundred-meter dash at the Paris Olympics because the early heats were scheduled to take place on the Sabbath. The full weight of the British Olympic Committee, including the Prince of Wales, crashed down on him, insisting he run for God and country. Liddle calmly refused. A classic upper-class English twit accused him of being arrogant. Nothing was further from the truth. His strength was rooted in humility, clearly knowing who he was. He did not run.

Humility Allows Us to Listen to Others

Because the humble don't always need to be right, it is easy for them to accept the advice and good counsel of others. One of the greatest gifts another person can give us is to ask, "What do you think?" Most of us operate within some sort of structure where we must take the direction of our "superiors," or face the consequences. These hierarchical relationships dominate our social and professional lives, whether it is that of supervisor/employee, teacher/student, parent/child, professional/client, or coach/athlete. Even in relationships of so-called equality—such as marriage or friendship or volunteer work—we often feel manipulated or coerced into accepting the decisions of others. Or we do what others want because we hope to get something from them. A humble person, however, is one who freely and gladly abides by the decisions of others.

My late friend B. J. Weber often recounted his own journey toward humility. In his early twenties, B. J. was totally out of control with drugs, sex, and violence. One day on a wanton road trip through eastern Iowa, he stopped at the New Melleray Abbey because he'd heard the monks there made great bread. He went in to buy a loaf . . . and stayed for seven years. Towards the end of his stay, he was in seminary, living at an adjacent convent, and working as a handyman for the nuns. The abbess, Columba Guare, was also his spiritual director at the time.

The story of B. J.'s conversion had spread through Christian channels, and one day he received a phone call from someone in the Billy Graham organization asking him to come and give his testimony at the next Graham crusade in Cincinnati. He couldn't believe it! But when he rushed in to tell Mother Columba that he was going to be able to tell his story in front of thousands of people and millions would see it on television, she was less than enthusiastic. "You can't go. It will just give you a fat head that will hinder your spiritual growth," she told him. "And besides, neither God nor Billy Graham need your help." B. J. was stunned. After a few moments of sullen silence, he responded, "I'm going." With a sweet smile Mother Columba replied, "That's fine. But then you will need to pack up your things and be out of here by 5:00 p.m."

Later, B. J. described this as the first great defining moment in his Christian life, because he clearly, soberly saw two paths open before him. One path honored his ego; the other path honored God. He did not go to Cincinnati. The crusade went fine without his testimony. And in those moments B. J. learned humility.

All of us are faced with moments like this. Usually we just act unconsciously, but sometimes we are given the grace to see the paths opening before us. Will we choose God, or will we choose our own ego? Will we choose God, or will we choose to indulge ourselves?

This points to the real genius of Christian humility. Ultimately, we are called to put aside our own agenda and seek to do God's will. A humble Christian doesn't do this out of a hope for reward, or to avoid punishment. Although humility leads to joy and a profound inner freedom, a humble Christian realizes those are just byproducts. When we become selfless—when we simply become open to what is around us and open to God—we actually become what God intends us to be. We become what we were created to be. We become our true selves.

The End of Humility

But you know what? That is not why God gives us humility. It is not an end in itself. God gives us humility for one reason only: for others. We can never forget that as people of faith, we live in two worlds. In our everyday existence, we live in a world of the senses, where we experience pleasure and satisfaction as well as pain, suffering, and anxiety. But as Christians we simultaneously live in another world, a world invisible to the senses but open to faith. That world is the kingdom of God. And it is the virtue of humility that enables us to become transparent, to become like windows or doorways between those two worlds. When we embrace humility—when we put down our own agenda, when in God's grace we become truly selfless—we allow God's love to come through us into the world.

It is through this state of humility and selflessness that we truly become the body of Christ. He is the head, but we are his hands and feet, the agents of God's redemption, so that "all who exalt themselves will be humbled, and all who humble themselves will be exalted" (Matt 23:12).

Humility is our vocation, one to which every Christian is called. As the Scottish theologian P. T. Fosyth (1848–1921) wrote, "Christianity is not the sacrifice we make, it is the sacrifice we trust. It is not the victory that we win, it is the victory that we inherit."[5] We will never know the full reality of God's redemptive love until we stand before God, like the hobbits and Strider, like Eric Liddle, with pride and self-absorption broken, acknowledging our weakness and God's strength revealed in Jesus Christ. In our weakness, in that humility, we will know the exaltation of God.

---

5. Forsyth, *Justification*, 220.

Chapter 2

Faith

> *Therefore, having been justified by faith, we have peace with God through our Lord Jesus Christ.* (Rom 5:1)

IN THE TWELFTH CHAPTER of Paul's First Letter to the Corinthians there is a very odd and peculiar passage: "No one can say 'Jesus is Lord' except by the Holy Spirit" (v. 3). The reason this has always struck me as strange is that on its surface the statement doesn't seem to be true. If I went out on any street corner with a hundred-dollar bill in my hand, waving that money above my head and declaring to all passersby that I would give it to them if they said, "Jesus is Lord," I have no doubt that many would say it simply to get the money. Obviously, anyone can make that statement without truly being inspired by the Holy Spirit.

So what does St. Paul really mean? Well, it's no mystery. What he really means is no one can *believe* that Jesus is Lord unless he or she is inspired by the Holy Spirit. No one can *know* that Jesus is Lord except by the Holy Spirit. His is a statement that goes far beyond acknowledging that Jesus a member of the nobility, or that he is some honored person; in the context of the Bible, to say "Jesus is Lord" is a declaration that he is God incarnate, that Jesus is Emmanuel, God among us. And that is something no human being can know or believe without the help of God, without the inspiration of the Holy Spirit. This is the truth that opens for us the mystery of faith. In reality, faith is an extremely complex phenomenon, with three distinct but complementary aspects. First, faith is assent to truth. Second, faith is trust—entrusting our well-being to another. And finally, faith is fidelity. Assent to truth, trust, and fidelity.

Faith as Assent to Truth

Nearly 250 years ago, Thomas Jefferson wrote in the Declaration of Independence, "We hold these truths to be self-evident, that all men are created equal, that they are endowed by their Creator with certain unalienable Rights, that among these are Life, Liberty and the pursuit of Happiness." This is a statement that some scholars have called the single most important sentence ever written, and certainly the most important in American history and society. Taken at face value, it declares every human being is equal under the law, because every human being has rights bestowed upon him or her by God. Almost every major change in the fabric of our society—from the abolition of slavery to voting rights for women, from desegregation of schools to gender equality in the workplace—has depended on belief in the truth of that statement. Do you believe it? Do you think that we are all created equal and every human being has rights that are given to us by God?

If you said yes, you made an act of faith, of faith as assent to truth. Faith begins with assent to the truth of certain principles. This is something we all do, all the time, mostly in non-religious, secular ways. Fundamentally, the social, moral, and political values of individuals in every society can seem mysterious on the surface, because they rest on faith as assent to truth. They are not, in spite of what Jefferson claimed, self-evident.

In truth, there are many people who don't believe that all people are created equal. When I've asked groups if they believe it, in the past about 90 percent of Americans have said yes. But I've asked the same question in Britain and Denmark, and almost no one in those countries—democracies like our own—believes it to be true.

The reality is that other societies do not have the same values of our own. One of the ironies of the 1970s was the debate on moral values between the American president Jimmy Carter and Leonid Brezhnev of the Soviet Union, which is mentioned in the introduction to this book. Carter publicly criticized the Soviet Union for denying individuals freedom of conscience, freedom of speech, freedom of assembly, and freedom of worship. The Soviet leader would have none of that, and roundly criticized America for denying individuals the right to universal healthcare, the right to universal education, and the right to employment. It is faith as assent to truth that creates social as well as individual values.

Religious Faith as Assent to Truth

The foundation of all religion is the assent to some accepted truth. Christian faith begins with assent to the truth of the gospel, the great metanarrative of redemption that is laid out in the Bible. This story has four basic components. First, it was God's intention in creation that human beings would live with God and one another in perfect intimacy, transparency, and love. Second, humanity (represented in Adam and Eve) rejected that intimacy in the sin of pride, in order to live as if they themselves were god. Third, since that original sin passed to all human beings and we cannot overcome either it or its consequences ourselves, God became incarnate in Jesus Christ, and through his death and resurrection our sins have been forgiven. And, finally, by putting our trust in Jesus Christ, we can enter into the kingdom of God, now and on into eternity. If you believe those things, it can only be through an act of faith as assent to truth.

But Christian faith also relies on assent to the theological truth of the gospel. We share much with other religions, especially Judaism and Islam, but there are four principles that make us Christian. It is also true that Christians disagree with one another about many things, such as the nature of authority, how we are to be accountable, and how we embrace salvation, but all Christians must assent to the truth of these four principles: the truth of the Trinity, that there is one God in three persons, Father, Son and Holy Spirit; the truth of the Incarnation, that God became human in Jesus Christ; the truth of the atonement, that in Jesus Christ our sins are forgiven; and the truth that through the Holy Spirit, God is redemptively active in the ongoing Christian community. Again, if you believe those things, it is through faith as assent to the truth.

But here's the rub. Understanding the truth of the gospel, whether it is narrative or theological, is easy. Believing it is hard, because there is nothing self-evident about it. Many can understand what it claims and don't believe it to be true. This is where God enters the picture, because we cannot create this belief in ourselves. Bill Gates isn't rich enough to buy it. Mother Theresa wasn't selfless enough to earn it. Albert Einstein wasn't smart enough to discover it. No, the only way anyone can believe the truth of the gospel is if the Holy Spirit gives that person faith as a free gift of grace.

No one in the twentieth century described this with more clarity than C. S. Lewis. A brilliant scholar and Oxford don, he was a professed and committed atheist as a young man. His conversion took place in two stages. Initially, he slowly came to believe in the existence of God. Then certainty came to him suddenly, while he was riding home on a bus. As he wrote in his memoir *Surprised by Joy*, "In the Trinity term of 1929 I gave in, and admitted that God was God, and knelt and prayed."[1] Still, he was far from being a Christian. He just couldn't accept the truth of the Gospels, that God became human in Jesus Christ, and that through his death and resurrection our sins are forgiven and we can enter eternal life. For Lewis, this was simply a retelling of the "myth of the corn king": the harvest myth told in dozens of ancient societies, that something or someone must die for new life to emerge.

Lewis's two great friends, Hugo Dyson and J. R. R. Tolkien, were passionate Christians. Late one night in September 1931 they all took a walk along the River Cherwell, from Magdalene College to the Oxford Zoo. When Lewis declared the Christian story is simply a version of the myth of the corn king, Tolkien agreed. But, he went on, the Christian story is also utterly unique, because unlike other myths of the corn king, it alone claims to have taken place in history. In some mysterious way, that was the tipping point for Lewis. "I have just passed on from believing in God to definitely believing in Christ—in Christianity," he wrote to his friend Arthur Greeves. "My long night talk with Dyson and Tolkien had a good deal to do with it. I know very well when . . . the final step was taken. When we set out, I did not believe that Jesus Christ is the Son of God, and when we reached the zoo, I did."[2] That belief, that assent to truth, was the gift of the Holy Spirit.

Do you agree with Lewis that Jesus Christ is the Son of God? If you can—with honesty, integrity, and passion—a miracle has already taken place in your heart and mind. Because there is nothing self-evident about the truth of those statements, those declarations; you can only say yes if God has given you the grace to assent to their truth. This is what Paul meant when he wrote, "No one can say 'Jesus is Lord' except by the Holy Spirit." If you can, thank God for the gift of faith. And if you hesitate, but desire it, ask God for the very same gift.

---

1. Lewis, *Surprised by Joy*, 228.
2. Lewis, *They Stand Together*, 45.

Faith as Trust

In Wendell Berry's wonderful novel *Jayber Crow*, the titular protagonist is a quiet, retiring man, a bachelor, and the town barber. But he is also a keen observer of life, and a man of deep and abiding Christian faith. As a matter of fact, he is a saint—although no one knows that, not even himself. After all, he's just a barber. "I am a man who has hoped that his life, when poured out at the end, would say, 'Good-good-good-good-good!' like a gallon jug of the prime local spirit," he reflects near the end of his life. "I am a man of great losses, regrets, and griefs. I am an old man full of love. I am a man of faith. But faith is not necessarily, or not soon, a resting place. Faith puts you out on a wide river in a little boat, in the fog, in the dark."[3] That is faith as trust.

This isn't so easy. It demands that we entrust our well-being to another by taking risks and becoming vulnerable. We all know what this primal act feels like. It is what newborn infants first learn as they reach out to the world around them, looking for some kind of contact, hoping to find not only the physical nurture they will need to survive, but also some kind of affinity, kinship, unity, and communion. Small children learn about this in relationship to their parents.

In March of 1994, my five-year-old son Andrew and I were going from our home in Millbrook, New York to Orlando, Florida so we could enjoy several days at Disney World. It was a trip fraught with difficulty. The day we left, a huge blizzard came roaring in from the west. In order to make our flight, we had to get up and leave the house by 4:00 a.m. and drive down to LaGuardia Airport with the blizzard chasing us the whole way. I was wracked with anxiety, while Andrew blissfully slept in the backseat. At the airport, the snow had already started falling and I fretted and fretted about what we would do if the airport closed. Andrew, meanwhile, continued to peacefully doze, even as we finally boarded the plane and took off. Once onboard, the pilot informed us that we were the last flight to take off before LaGuardia shut down. But we weren't out of the woods; we still had to change planes in Washington, where a sleet and ice storm was moving in. But again, we managed to get out just before that airport closed. Only then did Andrew fully wake up in the seat next to me. I had been wrestling with worry and anxiety for hours, but he remained ignorantly confident I would get him to Orlando safely and on time. Children know about faith as trust.

---

3. Berry, *Jayber Crow*, 356.

As children grow up, this trusting vulnerability is challenged by friends, classmates, and teachers. When we become vulnerable, and are affirmed and nurtured, our trust grows. But when our vulnerability is confronted with neglect or abuse or rejection, our trust is destroyed. Sometimes we make ourselves vulnerable to people or even institutions that disappoint, hurt, and discard us. We all know people who have entrusted themselves to individuals who are wanton and callous, or even to institutions that are unworthy. In 1987 I became rector of Grace Church in Millbrook, New York. Millbrook is in Dutchess County, in the Mid-Hudson Valley, population two hundred thousand. About thirty thousand of those people worked for IBM, and about another fifteen thousand worked for IBM suppliers. That meant close to half of the workforce depended on IBM.

That included several dozen of my parishioners. Many of them had been offered better jobs with higher salaries by other companies, but they remained loyal to IBM because along with other benefits the company promised lifetime employment. But in spite of a generation of promises, by 1992 the company had eliminated twenty thousand jobs in the county. Many of those people, including several of my parishioners, felt betrayed. They had entrusted themselves to an institution that proved unworthy of their trust. They would never allow themselves to be so vulnerable again.

Have you ever been betrayed by an institution, or by a friend or family member? The consequence is pain and heartache, which often leads to shutting down emotionally and withdrawing into ourselves. Every human being knows what faith as trust feels like, and what it feels like to lose it.

Religious Faith as Trust

To be a person of Christian faith means that regardless of our circumstances, we are willing to trust in Jesus, in God, for our happiness, security, and welfare. Sometimes this is instinctual. There is a person who is very close to me who scorned faith during the entire time I knew him. Anyone who would turn to God for help in the midst of a crisis, he felt, was a weakling. He insisted that he, and he alone, could deal with any problem he had. Once, after skiing together in the Berkshires, we began to drive home after dark in a snowstorm. We were on a twisty two-lane highway, and the road was slick and dangerous. At one point, I lost control of the car and we went into a complete 360-degree spin, crossing right through the oncoming traffic before landing in a snowbank on the other side of the highway. It was all over in just a few seconds, but as we sailed through traffic completely out of control, my scornful agnostic friend cried out at the top of his lungs, "Lord Jesus, save me!"

Sitting in the car, panting, with adrenaline flowing, I remarked, "I thought only weaklings turned to God when they were in trouble?" He spat back, "Shut up." The memory puts a smile on my face every time I've seen him since. Because I'm more than happy to remind him of it.

For most, faith in God is learned behavior. The last two years in seminary, I served as youth minister at St. Paul's Congregational Church in Claremont, California. There was a pretty sixteen-year-old girl named Betsy who was a member of the youth group. She didn't come very often, and I didn't know her well. Then one Sunday she arrived with her left eye swollen. When I asked what had happened, she said her dog scratched her. Well, the bulging increased dramatically over the next couple of days until her mother finally took her to see a doctor. They ran some tests, and on Thursday afternoon her mother called to tell me that they had discovered a malignant tumor behind her eye. The doctor advised them that the only treatment was to surgically remove the entire eye socket. She asked if I would come right over to their house to be with them.

I panicked. I had absolutely no clue what I could say to Betsy and her mother. What do you say to a beautiful sixteen-year-old who is going to be physically disfigured, and may still die? I felt completely helpless, with absolutely no idea what to say. But I knew someone who would know. Our senior minister, Joseph Applegate, had been in parish ministry for over fifty years, and had experienced everything. He would know exactly what to say. So I drove over to his house before going on to see Betsy. As I sat with him and explained the situation and asked his advice, he replied, "I have no idea what to say. I have never known what to say in situations like that."

I couldn't believe it. "Joseph, you have to help me," I told him. "I mean it. I don't know what to do." He repeated, "I have no idea what you should say." I was furious, convinced that he knew what to do but just wasn't telling me. So I stormed out, jumped in my car, and sped over to Betsy's house, where I parked the car and simply sat in it for about twenty minutes. I still didn't know what to say. I prayed, railing, demanding God show me what to do. Silence. Finally, I pulled myself out of the car, still praying, and went in not knowing what to say to Betsy or her mother. I just cried with them, held them, got angry alongside them, prayed with them. I spent hours with them before the surgery, and in the days after.

Betsy confronted her circumstances with remarkable courage and grace. After the surgery she took to wearing colorful eye patches that made her look exotic and mysterious. She had her first real boyfriend. She finished her junior year of high school with great grades. And then, in June, the cancer came back. I was with her in the hospital the day before she died. She told me she was ready. She was at peace. From that time forward, whenever I find myself in a situation where I don't know what to say or what to do, I offer a prayer of thanks to God for Joseph Applegate. Because he had the wisdom to not offer formulas or platitudes, and he had the wisdom to know that if I stood before God with nothing, God would be with me, blessing me, showing me, without my even being conscious of it, just what to say and do.

God's people, those who understand faith as trust, have always known this. That's what the psalmist was thinking when he wrote,

> In you, O LORD, have I taken refuge; let me never be ashamed. In your righteousness, deliver me and set me free; incline your ear to me and save me.
>
> Be my strong rock, a castle to keep me safe; you are my crag and my stronghold. Deliver me, my God, from the hand of the wicked; from the clutches of the evildoer and the oppressor. For you are my hope, O Lord God, my confidence since I was young. (Ps 71:1–5)

The next time you find yourself at the end of your rope—whether you're dealing with an illness, or a financial crisis, or a broken relationship, or the death of a loved one—remember that we are called to entrust our well-being to God. God doesn't promise to change our circumstances, but God does promise to be with us, and sustain us with divine strength, divine courage, and divine patience.

Faith as Fidelity

One of the most astonishing aspects of the Bible is the fact that so many of its heroes were people of no significance. It's true that some were endowed with greatness, people like Moses, Elijah, Sampson, David, and Solomon. But look carefully at others who pushed forward God's plan of salvation. There was nothing particularly outstanding about Abraham. As a matter of fact, he was a coward and a liar. Still, he was the single human being who received God's promise of salvation. Or take Jacob, a deceitful swindler.

He became Israel. Or Ruth, an inconsequential Moabite, who became the mother of Jesse, and the matriarch of the Messiah. Or Gideon, who—by his own estimation—was nothing, telling the Angel of the Lord that his clan was the weakest in Manasseh, his family the feeblest in his clan, and that he was the least in his family.

Yet Gideon—this weak, inconsequential, feeble shepherd from the backwaters of Palestine—rallied the tribes of Israel into a potent force that cast off the oppressive yoke of the mighty Mideonites. And then he ruled Israel with wisdom and grace for a generation as the nation's judge, a tenure marked by prosperity and peace. There was one thing all these flawed people shared—Abraham and Jacob, and Ruth and Gideon. It was faith as fidelity to the will of God.

If faith as trust is like a child's trust in her parents, fidelity is faith in the commitment of free, responsible adults. The primary definition of "fidelity" in the *Oxford English Dictionary* is "faithfulness." We have all met people whose lives are marked by fidelity, people who commit themselves to a way of life, and are determined to follow that commitment to the end. We all know people who have struggled to save a bad marriage, who have nursed the dying with love and concern, who are always there for us when we are in need. The people I most admire are those who consistently display fidelity, and those I least admire are those who never follow through on commitments, whose lives are marked by infidelity.

Faith as Fidelity to God

As Christians we are called to be a people of fidelity, faithful to God. Not just part of the time, not just when things are going well, but all the time, under any circumstances, right to the end of our lives. This understanding was codified in the covenant between God and Israel: "I will be your God and you will be my people" (Gen 17:7). It is seen in the first of the Ten Commandments: "You shall have no other gods before me" (Exod 20:3). According to Jesus, the greatest commandment was clear: "You shall love the Lord your God with all your heart, mind, soul and strength; and you shall love your neighbor as yourself" (Matt 22:27). And in this fidelity, we are called to persevere to the end. Time and again, St. Paul writes about running the race, fighting the good fight, seeing the finish line, and pressing on until the race is over. "Those who endure to the end will be saved," Jesus said (Matt 24:13). To live the Christian life is to respond to God with fidelity and commitment.

St. Paul certainly manifested fidelity in his own life. As he wrote to the Corinthians:

> I have worked much harder, been in prison more frequently, been flogged more severely, and been exposed to death again and again. Five times I received from the Jews the forty lashes minus one. Three times I was beaten with rods, once I was pelted with stones, three times I was shipwrecked, I spent a night and a day in the open sea. I have been constantly on the move. I have been in danger from rivers, in danger from bandits, in danger from my own people, in danger from Gentiles; in danger in the city, in danger in the country, in danger at sea; and in danger from false believers. I have labored and toiled and have often gone without sleep; I have known hunger and thirst and have often gone without food; I have been cold and naked. (2 Cor 11:23–27)

Yet with fidelity, he persevered to the end.

This kind of fidelity is not unique to New Testament Christians. In the early 1970s, after the war in Vietnam ended, dozens of servicemen were left behind as prisoners of war. For several years, nobody knew whether those men were dead or alive. There were rumors about terrible punishment, even torture. It was especially difficult for the families back in the United States, who had no way of knowing whether their husbands, fathers, or sons were still living, or what kind of condition they were in.

Finally, in 1975 the Vietnamese government allowed the POWs to write home to their families. As I heard in a sermon,[4] there was a woman in Kansas who had been waiting for two years when she finally received a letter. She immediately recognized her husband's handwriting, and her heart soared. He was alive. She sat down, calmed herself, opened the letter, and immediately her heart sank: the Vietnamese censors had blacked out all but a few words. She knew he was alive, but she had no idea whether he was well or sick, at peace or in despair. In frustration and grief, she cried, fretfulling turning the envelope over and over in her hands. Then she noticed something strange: the place where there should have been her zip code was something the Vietnamese censors had missed. It read, "2 COR

---

4. Sermon delivered by Neil Swanson at the Makawao Union Church, November 1977.

1–8-11." She sensed this was something significant, but had no idea what it meant. Then something popped into her mind.

She went to her Bible and opened it to 2 Corinthians, chapter 1, verses 8–11 and read these words:

> We do not want you to be unaware, brothers and sisters, of the afflictions we experienced in Asia. For we were so utterly, unbearably crushed that we despaired of life itself. Indeed, we felt that we had received a sentence of death, so that we could not rely on ourselves, but on God who raises the dead. He who rescued us from so deadly a peril will continue to rescue us. On Him we have set our hope that he will rescue us again, and that you will also join in helping us by your prayers.

Her heart again soared, through the words of St. Paul. She knew her husband was well. His faith would sustain him.

Where does such fidelity come from? For me, this has always been the most difficult aspect of faith. In grace, I have found it easy to assent to truth, and in crisis easy to entrust my well-being to God. But even as I know God's will—summarized in the Great Commandment, "Love God, and love your neighbor"—I have consistently faltered, stumbled, and even sometimes fallen flat on my face in my inability to do that to which God has called me. Those failures are constant reminders of my need for grace.

Because true fidelity can only be found as a gift of grace given to us freely by God. We must first be conscious that it is what God wants for us. And then we must be prayerful in asking God to sustain us.

Ultimately It Is Not Our Faith

Faith is the heartbeat of the Christian life, a complex combination of assent to truth and trust, crowned with fidelity. And it is ours for the asking. The Bible promises that if we turn to the Father, God will sustain us. That is why St. Paul could write in the eighth chapter of his Letter to the Romans,

> If God is for us, who can be against us? Who will separate us from the love of Christ? Will hardship, or distress, or persecution, or famine, or nakedness, or peril, or sword? No, in all these things we are more than conquerors through him who loved us. For I am convinced that neither death, nor life, nor angels, nor rulers, not things present, nor things to come, nor powers, nor height, nor

depth, nor anything else in all creation shall separate us from the love of God in Christ Jesus our Lord. (Rom 8:31, 35–39)

This is the heart of the Christian mystery. It is not our faith that leads us to the truth. It is not our faith that sustains us in time of peril. It is not our faith that carries us to the end. It is Jesus' faith. Jesus is our truth, our trust, our fidelity, and it is in him we are saved, in him we will find our faith. As he said to his disciples, "And remember, I am with you always, even to the end of the age" (Matt 28:20).

Chapter 3
Hope

But this I call to mind, and therefore I have hope: The steadfast love of the LORD never ceases, his mercies never come to an end; they are new every morning; great is your faithfulness. "The LORD is my portion," says my soul, "therefore I will hope in him." (Lam 3:21–24)

And not only that, but we also boast in our sufferings, knowing that suffering produces endurance, and endurance produces character, and character produces hope, and hope does not disappoint us, because God's love has been poured into our hearts through the Holy Spirit that has been given to us. (Rom 5:3–5)

IN THE WINTER OF 1983, I went to a meeting in New York City that had been called to organize support for a new mission in Bolivia called Amistad. One of the people I met there I will call Will Carpenter. Will was a managing partner at a major investment bank. He was the epitome of a successful Wall Street banker: icily cool and supremely confident. We both joined the board of the new mission, and as we worked together over the next few years, mutual respect developed into a friendship.

One day, Will called to tell me that his oldest son, also named Will, was in Columbia Presbyterian Hospital. I had only met young Will once. He was in his late twenties, and also worked on Wall Street, a young hotshot with his whole career ahead of him, already supremely confident about his life and his accomplishments. The doctors suspected he had cancer. Will Sr. asked if I would go with him to visit his son.

At the time, no one knew the extent of the cancer. It was before the common use of MRIs. Young Will's legs had swelled up, and twice blood clots had entered his lungs. On both occasions he almost died, and although he managed to pull through, his doctors knew that there was cancer growing someplace inside of him. They just didn't know where it was. I didn't know why Will Sr. wanted me to be there, because he didn't let me say anything at all. I just sat with them while he talked to his son.

He wanted his son to know that he had come to a new faith in God. Will Sr. shared that he had experienced God's love in such a tangible way, he knew all of life was in God's hands. He couldn't explain to his son why this was, but he just knew. He was absolutely certain.

Young Will was a skeptic. His only concern was getting out of the hospital, and getting on with his life. But as he got sicker and sicker, and they still could not isolate the cancer, I would visit him about once a week. One day when he was getting very frustrated, he said to me, "You know, Ken, I only ask for one thing. I only need a little window of hope. I know that if they just give me a little ray of hope, I can fight this thing." I was there when the oncologist came and told him what they had discovered—the cancer was in his liver, and it had already begun to metastasize. The doctor looked him in the eye and said there was nothing more they could do. There was no treatment. Will was given between two and four months to live. He had been given absolutely no hope.

Where Can We Find Hope?

That story is analogous to that of Moses receiving the Law of God on Mount Sinai. We know the story of the exodus; how God called Moses and sent him down into Egypt to liberate the people of Israel. Finally, after Moses brought down ten plagues, the Egyptians let the Israelites go. When Moses miraculously parted the waters, they passed through the Red Sea. The miracles continued as God was with them in the wilderness, sustaining them with manna from heaven, providing water in desolate desert places for their thirst, and quail for their hunger. God guided them as a pillar of fire by night and a cloud by day.

Then God called the people to Mount Sinai. Through Moses, God told the Israelites that God wanted to make a covenant with them: "Now therefore, if you obey my voice and keep my covenant, you shall be my treasured possession out of all the peoples. Indeed, the whole earth is mine, but you shall be for me a priestly kingdom and a holy nation" (Exod 19:5–6). The people of Israel agreed, entering into this special relationship with God, a covenant of mutual fidelity. Then—as a sign of this relationship, as a sign of the fidelity between God and Israel—God gave Moses the Law. This was to be their guide in living out their promise to be God's people.

So what happened? Almost immediately God's chosen people made a golden calf, which they began to worship in God's place. Within days of their promise, they had broken the covenant. God's judgment was swift and the idolaters were destroyed.

At that point, God called Moses back to the peak of Mount Sinai. Can you imagine how Moses felt? To be summoned by God after his community had violated the covenant, the promise of fidelity? He must have been filled with dread and terror.

But when he got to the top of the mountain to face God, Moses received a gift that no human being had experienced before. It was that God's promise of salvation did not depend on the faithfulness of Israel. The promise of salvation was founded on God's own faithfulness. Regardless of what the Israelites did, God remained true and steadfast to the promise. Moses experienced this when he looked into the heart of God, and saw that God's love would cover the sins of all humanity. When he came off the mountain, his face shone with the glory of God. It was so radiant that Moses was compelled to cover his face when he reported to the people of Israel. Again and again, he climbed the mountain with face uncovered, returning with his face alight with the knowledge that God is faithful even as we are unfaithful.

A very similar thing happened just before Jesus went to Jerusalem for the final time. Only he knew why he was going to Jerusalem: to fulfill the promise God made to Abraham. And only Jesus knew how that promise would be fulfilled: by taking the sin of the world upon himself. He was going to fulfill God's promise by dying in our place—a fearsome prospect.

Like Moses before him, Jesus climbed a mountain, bringing James and John and Peter with him. On top of the mountain, as his disciples watched, Jesus was transfigured. They couldn't really describe what they saw, but it was as if his robe became whiter than white, and the light and glory of God shone through him. Two people appeared with Jesus: Elijah and Moses, talking with him about what is going to take place in Jerusalem. They were talking with him about the crucifixion. They were talking with him about how his sacrifice would fulfill God's promise of salvation. In this knowledge, Jesus himself entered fully into the heart of God his Father. He knew that in spite of the terror of death and the pain of the crucifixion, he could approach his destiny with hope. He knew that his Father is faithful. The glory of this knowledge shone from him. Knowledge of God's love and fidelity is what caused Moses' face to radiate on Mount Sinai. Peter and James and John witnessed that glory through Jesus on the Mount of Transfiguration.

The Reality of Hope

It is important to know that there is a great difference between optimism and hope. Moses and Jesus had been given hope by embracing God's promise of salvation. But optimism is human centered. An optimist is a kind of person who when confronted with difficult circumstances, feels that he or she has the power to change those circumstances, or that other people will do it for them. Optimism is the belief in the power of human beings to change bad circumstances. That's not hope. Hope is the knowledge of God's love. In spite of our circumstances, God is in control of history, and the destiny of every human being. Hope has nothing to do with changing circumstances. Hope is what carried Jesus through the crucifixion. Hope gives us the knowledge that God will be with us no matter what.

The sin of despair is the absence of hope, the conviction that one's circumstances will never get better, that things will never change. It is a sin because it denies that God is in control of our destiny. Christian hope rests on the faith that our life—our future, our personal history—ends in the redemptive love of God. So whether we hope or despair depends on how we understand time and eternity, and in how we relate to the future.

Hope and Time

We live in time, experiencing reality sequentially. We know the past, we are fleetingly in the present, and the future remains a mystery. Though we can often predict the future with some probability based on past experience, certainty of the future remains unknowable. Hope determines how we face the future. In a secular sense hope is like optimism: the expectation that our desires will be realized, that they will come to pass in the future.

There is also false hope, a kind of Pollyannaish blind conviction that everything will turn out alright. We all know that is not true, unfortunately: loved ones will die, marriages will end in divorce, finances will collapse, and children will suffer at the hands of others. Yet there have been entire intellectual systems predicated on this kind of hope. The central tenet of Marxism is the inevitability of an economic utopia. American Progressivism as articulated by John Dewey taught that through education and hard work, all of society's problems could be resolved. Although that vision dominated American public education for over a century, the hard lessons of the twentieth century have left both it and the credibility of Marxism in tatters. On a personal level, books like *The Power of Positive Thinking* by Norman Vincent Peale have sold millions of copies, and influenced millions more to act with optimism.

Christian hope is very different. It has nothing to do with the fulfillment of our own desires. Rather, the object of Christian hope is the consummation of God's love in Jesus Christ. In faith we embrace the promise of salvation that God gave first to Abraham, which Moses experienced on Mount Sinai, and was fulfilled in Jesus Christ. But in spite of Jesus' death and resurrection, we still live in a world shot through with strife, conflict, and evil. Our hope is in the future promise that Jesus will come again. When? In the Second Coming, at the end of history. That coming will inaugurate the resurrection of the dead, Judgment Day, and the re-creation of heaven and earth. It is in this consummation, the apostle John wrote in the book of Revelation, when "every tear will be wiped away" (Rev 21:4).

This relationship to time is at the heart of Christian faith. It's why in the eucharistic we declare together, "Christ has died, Christ is risen, Christ will come again." Past, present, and future. It's why the Nicene Creed refers twice to the future: "He will come again in glory to judge the living and the dead, and his kingdom will have no end"; and, "We look for the resurrection of the dead, and the life of the world to come." In pondering this St. Paul wrote to the Corinthians, "Although now we see darkly, then we will see face to face" (1 Cor 13:12). It is in this consummation that all conflict and turmoil will be resolved. That is the hope that comes to us from the future.

Once, many years ago, when our daughter Katrina was about six years old, we were at our home in the Catskills, and she went to play at a neighbor's house. Her friend's father called to say he wanted to take the girls swimming at the local pool. When his pickup pulled up to the house with three little girls in the back, Katrina climbed out to change into her swimming suit, and the truck roared off. She was sure she was being ditched. And, as only a six-year-old can, she became hysterical, and completely inconsolable. This whole thing was a joke on her, a conspiracy. Her friends had plotted this just to hurt her feelings. She was completely caught up in this moment of despair.

In trying to reassure her, I did not enter into her despair. Because I knew something she didn't know. While she was locked into a moment of time that felt horrible, I had the advantage of looking at what happened from outside that moment, over the scope of an entire lifetime. I knew she would feel better in about a half hour, and she would be herself again by evening. Soon, she probably wouldn't even remember this incident, and by the time she was fifty, it would be insignificant. I knew that this wasn't an important moment in the whole scope of her life, so, in consoling Katrina, I could bring her hope. It was hard for her to see it at that moment, but because of my clear sense of resolution in the future, the hope was real.

As it turned out, even while we were talking, her friend's dad's pickup came blasting back. He had gone to drop off the other girl so she could change, and had returned for Katrina.

Christian Hope

Why is that like Christian hope? We live in time, but God does not. We experience reality sequentially with the known past, the fleeting present and the opaque future. But God sees all of history as a single moment. When God looks at you right now, God doesn't just see you in that moment; God sees your whole life, from birth to death. More than that, when God looks at you today, God doesn't just see your whole life. God sees the whole of your parents', grandparents', and great-grandparent's lives. God sees your children's, grandchildren's, and even your unborn great-grandchildren's lives. God sees all history as one moment, as one event.

Part of the wonder of the incarnation is that God the Son left his existence outside of time and entered history. He became bound like we are in time and space. And part of the wonder of the ascension is that after his resurrection from the dead, Jesus returned to eternity, to existence outside of time. From our perspective—existing in time, experiencing reality sequentially—where is Jesus right now? He is at the end of history, outside of time. He is already at Judgment Day. He is already at the resurrection of all humanity. He is already at the re-creation of heaven and earth.

That's why when God is present to us in faith, we experience peace and joy and love and—more than anything else—hope. When God comes to us in times of need, it's from a place out of time. God sees all of humanity and knows that what we are experiencing in the present is not the last word. God comes from a place where all things are resolved, and with the knowledge that every tear will be wiped away. God comes to us with the knowledge that because of Jesus' death on the cross, our sins will be forgiven and we will stand in the resurrection. When God comes to us in the midst of our need, God brings us hope. It is a hope grounded in God's love, which liberates us from our circumstances.

The Fruit of Hope

Hope is not an end in itself, but it provides peace and courage for us when we are most in need. Because, first and foremost, hope shatters despair. Young Will Carpenter—dying of cancer, with no place else to turn—turned to God. He asked God to give him the hope the oncologist had denied him. After his terminal diagnosis, before the day was out, his father had found other doctors who would treat his cancer. With treatment, the cancer went into remission, and he began to live his life with a new sense of vitality. He still had cancer, but his life was filled with hope.

Four months after the diagnosis, Will was married. I was deeply honored to perform the wedding. In my own heart and mind, it stands as the greatest symbol of hope I've ever experienced. Will returned to his career, working fruitfully. He and his wife began building a wonderful marriage together. And then the cancer came back. I was with him the day before he died. The circumstances could not have been more different than they had been eighteen months earlier. Even face-to-face with death, Will was filled with hope, with certainty that he could trust himself to God.

Hope also shatters hardness of heart. A person with a hardened heart already knows everything, knows all the answers. People with hardened hearts often find their deepest identity in commitment to -isms. Racism, because they *know* their race is superior. Sexism, because they *know* their sex should dominate. Dogmatism, because they *know* their particular beliefs are the truth. Moralism, because they *know* their way of living is righteous. Denominationalism, because they *know* their church is the most pure.

People with hardened hearts don't need to change, because they have already arrived. But if God is already at the end of history—and all things there are already resolved in God's redemptive love—hope obliterates hardness of heart, because the future belongs to God, not our -isms. And if the future belongs to God, we must become vulnerable and open to change in order to receive the future.

Hope also sets us free to be witnesses for justice. In our time, no one understood this better than Martin Luther King Jr. It would have been so easy for him to slide into the comfort of being the minister of a prominent church, unbothered by the racist structures of society, never having to confront hostility and violence. But what was it he declared? "I have been to the mountaintop and I have seen the Promised Land." What King meant was that in God's grace, he saw the end of history. He saw the consummation of God's promise to redeem humanity. He saw the Second Coming. He looked into the heart of God, and he saw that when all things are resolved in redemptive love, there is no racism. Does hope change our circumstances? No. But hope sets us free so that we can enter the world and establish God's justice.

Hope also enables us to enter into a state of joy. We are rarely conscious of this, but God created us for joy. This joy is what was lost in the fall. And joy is what Jesus came to restore. As he declared in John's Gospel, "I have said these things to you so that my joy may be in you, and your joy may be complete" (John 15:11). In his *Confessions* St. Augustine wrote that inside every human being is a God-shaped vacuum. That void has a strong longing to be filled. We spend much of our lives trying to fill the emptiness, cramming in possessions and relationships, achievements and pleasure. But, ultimately, none of those things will satisfy us. Why? Because it is a God-shaped vacuum. Only God can fill all its nooks and crannies. And when God does, we know the meaning of hope and fullness of joy.

Finally, hope enables us to know peace. In chapter 6 I describe peace as not the end of strife or violence, but rather an inner sense of wholeness and well-being that shatters guilt, anger, envy, anxiety, compulsion, dissatisfaction, frustration, and the pain of rejection and alienation. Through faith we can enter the timeless future at the end of history right now through a relationship with God, and hope will fill our entire being with goodness, tranquility, and harmony.

Seeking Hope

Is hope something you desire? Every one of us faces difficult circumstances. Sometimes it seems like they are going to crush us. Often in those times of need, optimism is foolish, but hope is not. Hope is the sure knowledge that

God is faithful even when we are not. Hope is what could lead St. Paul to say, "I know that all things work for good for those who love God" (Rom 8:28).

It is a certainty that grows out of an acceptance of God's love. The promise isn't that God will change our circumstances, but that God will bring us hope, a hope that will liberate us and enable us to live our lives productively and redemptively, a hope that is not based on us—not on our courage, or on our strength, or on our intelligence, or on our faith. It is a hope that rests on one thing and one thing alone: that God is faithful, and God will see the promise to its fulfillment and consummation. Because in the reality of God, outside of time, it has already happened.

Chapter 4

Agape

> *I give you a new commandment, that you love one another. Just as I have loved you, you also should love one another. By this everyone will know that you are my disciples, if you have love for one another.* (John 13:34–35)

IN ENGLISH, "LOVE" MAY be the most ambivalent, mushiest, and least precise word of any in the language. What exactly does it mean to love? I can say, "I love my wife," "I love my mother," "I love my dog," "I love to play golf," "I love ice cream," "She's falling in love." Someone can invite me to a party and I can respond, "I'd love to come." At that party someone might insult me, causing me to comment, "I'd love to punch that guy in the nose." We call sex "making love." We can even call one another "love." I used the word "love" ten times in this paragraph, and each time I meant something different.

This may not seem like a critical distinction. For you, ambivalence concerning love may not be an issue. But this a problem for Christians, because the entire requirement for a righteous existence is summed up by Jesus: "You shall love the Lord your God with all your heart, and with all your soul, and with all your mind, and with all your strength; and you shall love your neighbor as yourself. There is no greater commandment than these" (Mark 12:30–31). That is it. These dual imperatives are all we have to do to fulfill God's intention for us. That is the Christian *telos*, our human destiny as well as the source of the deepest human meaning. But if that is all, we had better understand exactly what "love" is, for it is God's greatest gift to humanity. As Paul wrote to the Corinthians,

If I speak in the tongues of mortals and of angels, but do not have love, I am a noisy gong or a clanging cymbal. And if I have prophetic powers, and understand all mysteries and all knowledge, and if I have all faith, so as to remove mountains, but do not have love, I am nothing. If I give away all my possessions, and if I hand over my body so that I may boast, but do not have love, I gain nothing. Love is patient; love is kind; love is not envious or boastful or arrogant or rude. It does not insist on its own way; it is not irritable or resentful; it does not rejoice in wrongdoing, but rejoices in the truth. It bears all things, believes all things, hopes all things, endures all things. Love never ends. But as for prophecies, they will come to an end; as for tongues, they will cease; as for knowledge, it will come to an end. For we know only in part, and we prophesy only in part; but when the complete comes, the partial will come to an end. When I was a child, I spoke like a child, I thought like a child, I reasoned like a child; when I became an adult, I put an end to childish ways. For now we see in a mirror, dimly, but then we will see face to face. Now I know only in part; then I will know fully, even as I have been fully known. And now faith, hope, and love abide, these three; and the greatest of these is love. (1 Cor 13)

Thinking Clearly about Love

Fortunately, there are languages far more exact than English in describing our inner lives. Greek, the language of the New Testament, has more than a dozen words, each with a unique and particular meaning, that are all translated into English as "love." For example, the word *hedone*, which has passed into English in words like "hedonism," is the Greek term for sexual love or the love of pleasure. *Storge* is instinctual affection, like what we feel when we see a baby or a puppy. That can also be used to describe the love between parents and children, although *eunoia* is specifically the love of parent for child. *Erasthai* and *aphrodisios* both mean to have a crush. And I could go on and on.

In Greek there are no fewer than three words that refer to an enriching, intimate love between individuals. *Philia* is the platonic love within families, and at the heart of deep friendship. It is the source of great contentment and well-being, and has passed into English in words like "filial," and most prominently in America in "Philadelphia," which literally means "brotherly love." Romantic love in Greek is *eros*. This is the word used to describe "falling in love" or "being in love." *Eros* is what Sammy Fain and

Paul Francis meant when they wrote the classic song "Love Is a Many-Splendored Thing." It obviously has a sexual component, as it has come into English in the words "erotic" and "eroticism." Poets have often plumbed its meaning as the source of both the deepest pain and soaring happiness human beings can experience.

Although *philia* and *eros* are distinct words in Greek, they share in common one very significant element: they are both conditional. Both demand, need, and expect—even when it is unconscious or unarticulated—to receive something in return from the object of their love. When we love someone with either *philia* or *eros* and don't get back what we need, the love we feel for that person withers.

Consider this: Have you ever fallen in love? Are you still in love with that first one, or the second, or the third? What happened? Did they let you down, or disappoint you, or reject you? The same is true with *philia*. If you've ever lost touch with an old friend, or been estranged from any member of your family, you'll be familiar with this. For most of us, friendships diminish and familial relationships are often strained. Why? Because our feelings change when our expectations and needs are unmet.

The New Testament, of course, was written in Greek. But none of the words I've detailed above is the one used in the New Testament to describe the love God has for us, or the imperative for us to love God and others. That word is *agape*. Like *eros* and *philia*, it is deeply intimate, and it leads to incredible bonding and intimacy. But unlike either *eros* or *philia*, *agape* is utterly, totally unconditional. When someone loves with *agape*, there is no requirement or expectation of anything in return. *Agape* is interested only in blessing and enriching the other. It has no concern for self. And it is not a natural love—many people have never experienced it. Others have known it only in fleeting moments of grace. But it is available to all of us.

Agape Accepts Others as They Are

Eros and *philia* are not only grounded in reciprocity; they very often demand familiarity or conformity: the conviction that other people be like us. The emotions of *eros* and *philia* can have a difficult time accommodating those who are different ethnically, socially, or racially, as well as those different politically, spiritually, or culturally. They demand comfort. With *agape*, on the other hand, we are willing to meet a person exactly where he or she is.

AGAPE

We all have certain obsessions, inclinations, and idiosyncrasies about which we might feel embarrassed if they were publicly known. For me, it is that when I was a boy and I got a new pair of shoes, as soon as I got home, I would go into my bedroom, shut the door, sit down on my bed, and hold my legs straight out so I could admire those shiny new shoes down there on my feet. When I was growing up in Wauwatosa, Wisconsin in the 1950s, it was an astonishingly homogeneous suburb. Almost everyone I knew was exactly like me, an upper-middle-class White Protestant. Our town's minority were the few Catholics. However, Wauwatosa bordered Milwaukee, and when I went into the city, I would often see people who were dramatically different.

Back then, Milwaukee was still a city full of first-generation immigrants, and the group who seemed most strange to me were elderly Polish grandmothers. They didn't speak English and they dressed in black from head to foot, wearing black woolen shawls, black woolen dresses, black woolen stockings, and black high-topped lace boots. As a self-absorbed adolescent, I couldn't be bothered with anyone who was different from me. I found people from whom I felt culturally alienated distasteful at best, and mildly threatening at worst. My usual response was simply to ignore them, trying to deny their very existence.

One day, when I was about fourteen, I had to take the bus downtown to visit my orthodontist. As I was sitting in a seat near the back, one of those old Polish grandmothers got on the bus and sat down directly opposite me. I paid her absolutely no heed. But after we had gone two or three stops, I noticed out of the corner of my eye that she had a sweet, almost beatific smile on her face. Intrigued, I looked more carefully. Sitting directly across from me, she was holding her legs straight out. She had on a brand-new shiny pair of high-topped black boots.

For me, this connection was a moment of grace, an intimation of *agape*, that forever shattered the comfort of my own tribal barriers. From then on, I knew that—in spite of language and culture and dress—strangers are actually not so different after all.

Growing up in Wauwatosa, I did not respond critically to my environment, and simply absorbed a great deal of hostility and suspicion toward Roman Catholics. As a young adult, after I had gone through a life-changing Christian renewal and became involved in ministry at the University of Wisconsin, I found myself in a rather awkward situation. For an event on campus several Christian groups were planning, I was assigned to go to seek support from Father Jim Egan, a Jesuit who directed the Catholic student center at the university.

Even though I was going to seek his support, I wanted him to be perfectly clear that I wasn't fooled by all that Roman Catholic superstition. You know, things like the cult of the Virgin and communion of the saints—that kind of stuff. I'd done a little reading. I knew what was really going on with their strange theology. So when I went to the Catholic center and I sat down in Jim Egan's office, before he had a chance to say anything, I was ready. I said, "You know this stuff about the Virgin Mary; historians are pretty much in agreement that before the time of Jesus, the dominant religious figure in the Mediterranean world was Isis, the mother goddess. And when those people became Christian, they just transferred all their devotion for the pagan goddess on to the Virgin Mary."

"Ha," I thought to myself, "what do you have to say to that?" I was ready for a fight. Jim Egan looked at me very carefully, and then a broad smile creased his face and he laughed out loud. He said, "Well, there's probably some truth in that. But Ken, I'm much more interested in you . . . and Jesus. Tell me about your relationship with Jesus." I was totally disarmed by his graciousness. He taught me something critically important that day: that the basis for love and unity between Christians—even Christians from radically different backgrounds, even Christians who harbor hostility—is Jesus. Jesus is the rock of our salvation and the ground of our unity. Not the Virgin Mary, not the Bible. Not when to do baptism, not dogma. Not the gifts of the Holy Spirit, not the authority of bishops. The basis for love and unity among Christians . . . is Jesus. But I only learned that because Jim Egan, with *agape*, accepted me just as I was, full of prejudice and all.

Agape Speaks the Truth in Love

We often find ourselves in situations in which we want neither to hear nor speak the truth. When someone important to us is behaving badly, we will often avoid addressing their harmful conduct. Maybe it's our boss, or a neighbor from whom we want a favor. Perhaps it's someone with whom we would like to have a romantic relationship, or a family member who can become intolerable when provoked. We don't want to jeopardize our relationships, or make ourselves vulnerable to rejection or retaliation. Sometimes we simply want to avoid confrontation, even with a stranger, so we bottle up our concern and indignation. We often ignore the truth, sometimes assiduously. *Agape* is a love that will not allow for such reticence.

In 1987, when I became rector of Grace Church in Millbrook, there was a woman in the parish who never spoke to me without being critical. I'll call her Betsy Green. There was never any affirmation for something I had done well—but if I ever did anything Betsy *didn't* like, she informed me quickly and clearly. After a while it really got to me. Sometimes I would wake up on Sunday morning wondering what it was she would say this time. When I was greeting people after church and I saw her coming, I braced myself. I knew I was in for it.

A couple of years later, I was in New York City at a diocesan meeting when another priest said to me, "Ken, I hear you're doing a great job in Millbrook." Pleased, I asked, "Who told you that?" He said it was Betsy Green! He then went on to detail all of the wonderful things she had told him about my ministry. I couldn't believe it. Driving home that night as I prayerfully thought about her, it dawned on me that what she had been doing was simply speaking the truth in love. She wasn't against me. She was for me. Every time she said something critical, it was because she wanted me to do better. She wanted the parish to become a stronger Christian community.

After that, when I saw her coming, I knew I was going to hear the truth. It might be painful, but it would be constructive. Soon, whenever faced with a difficult problem, I sought Betsy out. I knew she wouldn't beat around the bush, but would speak the truth in *agape*.

Agape Makes Us Listen

Many of us, much of the time, just don't listen. Sometimes that's because of pride—we think we already know it all. But more often, we don't listen because we're afraid of being vulnerable. To really listen to another person, you have to let them in close. I have a friend in New York who is outspokenly atheist: you don't have to ask if she believes in God; she'll find a way to tell you. One evening, as we were seated next to one another at a dinner party, the conversation turned toward faith. I was actually talking to someone else when she grabbed my arm and practically shouted, "Stop!" "What do you mean?" I asked. "I don't want to hear it," she said. "I've already made up my mind that there's no God. It makes me crazy to have to think about it. Just drop the whole thing."

Another reason we don't listen is because we want to stay in control. I particularly notice this when someone finds their own belief system or their own identity challenged. When someone says something that makes us angry, it is much easier to simply objectify, marginalize, and dismiss them than to try and understand why they said it. "He's an idiot." "He's a fascist." "She's a commie." And even if we don't say it, we think it. By objectifying others, we separate ourselves from them. We don't have to take them seriously or listen to them. And we stay in control.

All of these reasons to not listen can be explained by one psychological and spiritual reality: we don't listen because we don't want to change. Even if we are unhappy with our circumstances, the prospect of change fills us with fear. So we don't listen. We know everything already; we don't want to be vulnerable; we want to stay in control; we fear change. This unwillingness to listen is a manifestation of our lack of love.

When confronted with something that we don't want to hear, a good listener will ask, "How did you come to that conclusion? Tell me why you believe that." Even when we're upset, listening forces us to admit we actually don't know it all. Listening makes us vulnerable, forcing us to lower our boundaries, and set aside our own agenda. Listening forces us to relinquish control. It opens us to change. Why is this so important for people of faith? Simple. It's because Jesus gave us only one commandment: we are to love. We are to love God and our neighbor. *Agape* begins with listening.

My friend Tom Pike was rector of Calvary St. George's Episcopal Church in New York City for nearly forty years. I'll never forget him once saying that the greatest joy a human being can experience is to be completely known by another. Not to *know* completely, but to *be known* completely—to trust another person so fully that you can become totally vulnerable with them. You can share everything: your deepest fears, your most bitter resentments, your highest hopes, your secret desires. To be utterly open, absolutely transparent. When we find a relationship like that, we know the deepest connection a human being can experience. But none of us will ever know that joy unless there is someone who is listening. It requires love to share deep intimacy with another. We can give this joy to another only if we are truly willing to listen to them. Truly listening is a key element in *agape*.

Agape also demands that in listening, we refrain from imposing our own agenda on others. About a dozen years ago I became pastorally involved in a very messy, difficult divorce. My friend had discovered that his wife had been having an affair, one that began even before they were married. He began to have doubts about the paternity of their child. When DNA testing revealed that he was not the father of their little girl, his anger and pain were tremendous. I spent a great deal of time with him, giving him the best support and counsel I could. Eventually he moved to California and we lost touch.

Then, about five years later, we bumped into each other in New York City. To my surprise, he was extremely angry with me. He said that when he was going through his divorce, I hadn't been there for him. I was more than a little defensive at first, but I didn't have to ask him what he meant because he was perfectly willing to tell me. "The whole time, you acted like the expert," he told me. "You were full of advice, but you had no idea what I was feeling. Do you know what I really needed from you? To ask, 'What are you feeling? What can I do for you?' I didn't need advice. I needed someone to listen, someone to help me see that God was there for me."

That's what Jesus meant when he said, "Love one another as I have loved you" (John 13:24). That's what *agape* is. *Agape* doesn't mean giving advice. *Agape* doesn't require expertise. No, *agape* has no agenda. *Agape* means meeting another person where they are, without demands, without conditions. It is utterly selfless.

I'm often struck by how we often don't even know those to whom we are the closest. For instance, spouses who really don't know each other. They may live in the same house, but they aren't truly intimate. Why? Because they don't take the time to listen. Parents fail to really know their children, and their children, in turn, don't really know their parents. If you have teenage or young adult children, do you know what their favorite song is? Do you know their hopes and dreams? All too often, we don't know these things because we never take the time to listen.

Here is my challenge to you: In the next week, take someone with whom you should be intimate—a spouse, or child, or close friend, or parent, or partner—and sit down with them and ask three questions: "What are the things that worry you, the fears you carry around deep inside? What are the things that give you contentment, that make you happy right now?" Finally, "What would you like your life to be like five years from now?" This person may be reluctant to share because real listening seems alien. But merely by asking these questions, we not only make ourselves vulnerable; we are freeing others to become vulnerable to us. It allows your relationship to move from alienation toward joy.

I have another challenge for you as well: When you find yourself reacting to someone who has upset you instead of dismissively labeling and objectifying that person so you don't have to listen, try to remind yourself to ask a few simple questions: "Why do you believe that? How did you arrive at that conclusion?" And allow yourself to listen. This simple response—listening rather than reacting—will make the world a better place. We are called to love, and love begins with listening.

Love Is the Center

When I was a priest at Grace Church in New York, a young couple whose wedding I had officiated a few years before asked if I would be willing to help resolve a dispute they were having with the wife's parents. The young wife was pregnant with her second child, but testing had revealed that the baby boy she was carrying had severe spina bifida. Both the upper spinal cord and the back of his head were open. If the fetus was taken to term and delivered, the doctors didn't think he would survive more than a few days, perhaps just hours. The young woman's parents wanted her to have an abortion, but she wasn't so sure. It was her son, and she was inclined to carry him to term.

The five of us met at the couple's apartment, and the conversation—though filled with passion—was not at all acrimonious. On the contrary, it was driven by respect and love. The young woman's parents simply wanted to lessen the pain they knew their daughter would experience. They felt that aborting a child that had no chance for a decent life would enable their daughter and her family to get on with the rest of their lives. "After all," her father insisted, "what's the point of bringing a child into the world who will never accomplish anything. It may be that his only experience will be pain." The young mother felt differently. "I could care less about accomplishment," she said. "Even if he only lives a few hours, I want him to experience love. I want him to know he is loved."

I always feel that my job in a situation like that is to help people understand the consequences of various options, so they can make an intelligent decision. But in that discussion I had a hard time biting my tongue. While I could fully appreciate the parents' concern—they wanted to spare their daughter pain—I was deeply moved by her understanding of what is of ultimate value in human life. She was right: at the end of day, it doesn't matter what we have accomplished. The size of your bank account is not going to matter. It's not going to matter whether or not you earned a PhD. It's not going to matter whether your house is nicer than mine. It's not going to matter that you were able to lower your handicap. If we believe the gospel, if we believe Jesus, what matters is that we loved and were loved.

Once, in Nashville, I had the tragic task of burying a father and daughter who had both died of cancer within hours of one another. I didn't know either of them well, and was amazed at the response to the father's life that appeared in the press after his death. He was a physician on the faculty at Vanderbilt Medical School, and was devoted to caring for needy patients at the old General Hospital.

At the burial, one of his closest friends told me that at one time, he figured everyone in East Nashville knew this doctor. He was kind and decent to his patients, and he so touched the lives of his students and his colleagues that they couldn't help but offer him tribute. He always acted quietly, and would have been embarrassed by their notice. But if we believe the gospel, if we believe Jesus, the legacy that will matter in the end is a legacy of love.

The young woman who was carrying the baby with spina bifida took the child to term, and he was born into this world. He lived here for less than two days, but for every moment he was held in the arms of either his mother or his father or his grandparents. As his mother told me on the day of his funeral, her son lived knowing nothing but love. That is the greatest gift a parent can give a child. That is the greatest gift we can give one another.

Agape Demands Action

The first Hindu missionary to the West was a man named Vivekananda. He made a huge media splash at the World Congress of Religions in Chicago in 1893. In his lecture he was very critical of the Christian missionary effort in India. Thousands of missionaries sent, millions of dollars spent, and relatively few Christian converts. And little wonder he declared:

> You Christians, who are so fond of sending out missionaries to save the soul of the heathen—why do you not try to save their bodies from starvation? In India, during the terrible famines, thousands died from hunger, yet you Christians did nothing. You erect churches all through India, but the crying evil in the East is not religion—they have religion enough—but it is bread that the suffering millions of burning India cry out for with parched throats. They ask us for bread, but we give them stones. It is an

insult to a starving people to offer them religion; it is an insult to a starving man to teach him metaphysics.[1]

In another essay Vivekananda was very frank: "India will never become Christian until we see Christians who love as Jesus loved."[2]

Agape by its own nature is an active practice, seeking to meet the needs of those in trouble or in pain. And when that happens, not only are those people blessed, but the act of love itself is a powerful witness to the world.

During the 1950s and 1960s the most acerbic social critic in Britain was Malcolm Muggeridge, the editor of *Punch*, and later a commentator on the BBC. He was so scathingly sarcastic, with such rapier-like wit, no one in public life wanted to challenge him. Then, in the mid-60s, Muggeridge was assigned by the BBC to make a documentary film about an unknown nun in Calcutta. The film, called *Something Beautiful for God*, had a remarkable "cinema verite" quality, because although Muggeridge never appeared on camera, his sour, biting commentary was a constant off-camera chorus.[3]

The documentary had two very powerful moments. In the first, the camera crew trailed this anonymous nun through the streets of Calcutta while she searched out dying, derelict men and women abandoned on the streets. She was Mother Teresa, and when in the film she found just such a man, curled up in the gutter, she bent down and gently rolled him over. As she took him in her arms and began to bathe the open sores on his face, Muggeridge's sharp voice broke in, "Ugh! That is disgusting. The man reeks. How can you possibly bear to even touch him?" Mother Teresa turned her glowing face to the camera. "Oh, you don't understand," she said. "Whenever I look into the face of a dying person, I see the face of Jesus looking back at me."

The second moment took place at the Sisters of Charity convent, in a large room used as a hospice for dying men and women. Each patient was attended by a nun, who cared for them, bathed them, held them, prayed for them, all so that each could die surrounded by dignity and love. But the film crew was having a crisis. The cinematographer insisted that the room was too dark. He needed to set up bright, hot lights, or the filming would simply be a waste, recording only a dark gray blur. The nuns quietly refused, saying that nothing could be done that would upset or distract their

---

1. Vivekananda, *Complete Works*, 493.
2. Vivekananda, *Complete Works*, 151.
3. Muggeridge, *Vintage*, 42.

patients. Finally, after more irate exchanges among the crew, the decision was made to shoot without lights.

In the film, there was an immediate cut to the crew reviewing that day's footage. When the scene in the hospice appeared on the screen, it was filled with a powerful glowing light. "This is impossible," declared the stunned voices, off camera. "What is going on?" "How could this have happened?" Noticeably missing was Muggeridge's grating sarcasm. He remained utterly silent.

Several months after the film was completed in 1969, Malcolm Muggeridge publicly announced he had become a Christian. For him, Vivekananda's challenge half a century earlier had been met. India, and the world, had witnessed Christians who loved as Jesus loved—with *agape*, a love that actively seeks out those in need, a love that not only brings comfort to the suffering, but bears powerful witness to the reality of the gospel.[4]

But what about you? If you self-identify as a Christian, is there anyone who would know you are Christian by your love? The next time you're confronted with someone who threatens your sense of comfort, remember that—in God's eyes—they are just like you. The next time you're confronted by someone in need, don't give advice. Listen. And know that as you seek to minister to those in need, that it in itself will bear witness to the reality of God. That is how we begin to fulfill Jesus's commandment, "Love one another as I have loved you . . . By this they will know you are my disciple, if you love one another" (John 13:34–35).

---

4. Muggeridge, *Vintage*, 42.

Chapter 5
Apatheia

If the Son shall make you free, you will be free indeed. (John 8:36)

AT THE HEART OF the Christian gospel is a message of hope based on two spiritual realities. The first is that human beings, subject to sin, are accountable to God. As Jesus said, "the gate is wide and the road is easy that leads to destruction, and there are many who take it" (Matt 7:13). The whole meaning of the gospel is that Jesus came to liberate us from the thrall of sin. "Truly, truly, I say to you, everyone who commits sin is a slave to sin. The slave does not continue in the house forever; the son continues forever. So if the Son makes you free, you will be free indeed" (John 8:34–36).

When we reflect on the destructive nature of sin, it makes perfect sense to speak of the wide path it carves. Jesus talked of another way, the way of the kingdom of God. The promise given to the people of Israel and fulfilled in Jesus is that in the kingdom of God there is no sin. In the kingdom of God there is no overwhelming anger, no enslaving fear, no irresistible gluttony. As the prophet Jeremiah wrote:

> "This is the covenant I will make with the house of Israel after that time," declares the Lord. "I will put my law in their minds and write it on their hearts. I will be their God, and they will be my people. No longer will a man teach his neighbor, or a man his brother, saying, *Know the Lord*, because they will all know me, from the least of them to the greatest,' declares the Lord. 'For I will forgive their wickedness and will remember their sins no more."
> (Jer 31:33–34)

In the kingdom of God, we are called to live in perfect freedom, not as an end in itself, but in order to know and love God, and truly love our neighbors. In seeking this freedom, there is a virtue to be sought from God, and nurtured through spiritual disciplines. It is *apatheia* (pronounced apa-theeia).

Are We Slaves or Free?

As Americans we are constantly told that we have been especially blessed with freedom and peace. In spite of the historical stain of slavery and systemic racism, today in the early the twenty-first century our entire society, from politically correct progressives on the left to libertarians and MAGA mavins on the right, champions individual rights. And most Americans enjoy not just freedom but the peace that comes from a deep sense of security. In spite of pockets of drug-fueled warfare both urban and rural, the vast majority of Americans never come close to experiencing the strife or terror that takes place regularly in Israel, or Darfur, or the Ukraine.

But are we Americans truly blessed with freedom and peace? Only in the most shallow sense: your neighbor with the new car may be outwardly content and comfortable, but that doesn't mean his inner life is either free or peaceful. We are all, at least part of the time, buffeted by emotions and impulses like anger, fear, and desire that enslave us, causing tremendous inner dissonance and pain.

Take anger, for instance. Recently I was at a Target store. It was in the middle of the afternoon and only one cash register was open, which meant there was a long line. Right in front of me was a woman with a four-year-old, who was out of control. The little girl wouldn't stay in line no matter what her mother tried to do. She kept running away and each time she came back it was with something she wanted her mother to buy: candy, a toy, batteries, even a women's magazine. The mother kept getting more and more frustrated. It was actually possible to see her anger rising until finally she exploded. Afterwards, the little girl was hysterical and the mother felt humiliated. As I watched that scene unfold, I felt tremendous sympathy for the mother. Anyone who is a parent has gone through experiences like that. I could understand exactly how she was feeling. I am sure you can as well.

There are other kinds of anger that capture us. There is an anger that just won't go away, lingering and festering, like something stuck in our teeth that we can't dislodge. Several years ago, I learned that another member of my faith community was bad-mouthing me in public. My immediate response was rage I could not shake. For at least two days, no matter what I was doing, the anger was always there, incessantly disturbing my conscious mind. I simply couldn't escape it. Have you ever had an experience like that? Then there are people who are perpetually enraged, people who if you push the wrong buttons will explode all over everyone around them. Consequently, everybody who knows them walks on eggshells. Do you know anyone like that? All of us, at least part of the time, are subject to anger.

Or consider fear. I find fear a very interesting phenomenon because I have no control over when fear or anxiety are going to come pouring into my consciousness. Sometimes I am amazed at the situations about which I get anxious.

I'm used to speaking in public, but there are times when anxiety over it simply overwhelms me. I remember several years ago I took a course in order to become a mentor for the program Education for Ministry. I was placed in a small group of about ten people, and our first assignment was to tell the others about ourselves, in less than five minutes. As we moved around the circle and it kept getting closer to my turn, I became more and more nervous. When the person next to me was talking, my heart was pounding and I had shortness of breath. Have you ever experienced anything like that? Probably so. Sometimes fear just captures us.

Let's ponder gluttony for just a second, especially as it manifests itself as desire. Have you ever been infatuated? Has there ever been a person that you wanted to have a relationship with so badly that it became obsessive? You just couldn't get them out of your mind? This kind of obsession can be very destructive, so much so that it's become a major theme in our culture. Think of Emma Bovery or Anna Karenina. In pondering this I am also reminded of Josef von Sternberg's iconic film *The Blue Angel*, where the esteemed professor performed by Emil Jannings utterly destroys his life obsessively pursuing a young dancer played by Marlene Dietrich.

There is another kind of desire that I think is far more pervasive and subtle, one less concerned with relationships than with material things, like possessions and success. It is an inner drive, an inner imperative, even if we're not conscious of it, that pushes us to reach some level of status and then scramble to maintain it—homes, cars, vacations. It's this compulsion that makes us grasp for that promotion, or run scared even to keep the job we already have. It creates an inner dissatisfaction so we are never completely happy or at peace. We are always looking beyond what we have and reaching for more. This desire, whether we acknowledge it or not, controls us. This kind of desire shapes the way we live our lives.

In this context, do you still think Americans are especially blessed with freedom and peace? Not in our inner lives, where we are all captive to our emotions and impulses. That is not what God wants for us. As a matter of fact, when Jesus spoke of coming to set us free, what he was referring to was not external. He was talking about inner freedom.

Apatheia

There is no single word in English that adequately depicts this Christian freedom, but the Greek word *apatheia* gets close. It's a word very few Americans are familiar with, so what does it mean? It has been filtered through time into the English word "apathy," and although *apatheia* does carry a sense of detachment, it couldn't be further from the meaning of the English word "apathy." On the contrary, it is about an inner freedom that allows us to feel and experience everything, free from any anxieties or hang-ups. There is no repression in *apatheia*. We can still feel angry, feel fear. We are conscious of desire, compulsion, and obsession. But these inner emotions and impulses have no hold on us. With *apatheia* we remain completely free. I like to describe *apatheia* as like being in Montana. You can see from horizon to horizon. *Apatheia* comes with a big sky. In *apatheia* one is conscious of everything but held by nothing.

The word *apatheia* does not appear in the New Testament—which might be troubling to some of you, but the word "Trinity" doesn't appear in the New Testament either. But in the same way the entire New Testament is shot through with a Trinitarian understanding of God, the teaching of Jesus presents us with *apatheia* time and time again. As a virtue, the concept was deeply valued by pagan philosophers, particularly Stoics and Neo-Platonists.[1] Christian teachers in the second century began to use it in reference to the freedom Jesus spoke about, and it burst into common usage in the fourth and fifth centuries through the teaching of the desert fathers. Christian mystics such as Anthony, Macarias, and Evagrius Ponticus believed that *apatheia* was the supreme Christian virtue to be prized beyond all others. They taught that truly living a Christian life began with *apatheia*.

---

1. See Plotinus, *Enneads* VI.8.

Apathiea and Anger

Did you know that in the entire New Testament Jesus only gets angry once? We tend to think that when Jesus scourged the temple and overturned the tables of the moneychangers, he must have been angry. Go back to the scripture. It never once mentions anger. He was acting righteously, against greed and injustice, but not out of anger.

The only time in the New Testament describes Jesus feeling anger is when Pharisees try to prevent him from healing a crippled man on the Sabbath.

> Again he entered the synagogue, and a man was there who had a withered hand. And they watched him, to see whether he would heal him on the sabbath, so that they might accuse him. And he said to the man who had the withered hand, "Come here." And he said to them, "Is it lawful on the sabbath to do good or to do harm, to save life or to kill?" But they were silent. And he looked around at them with anger, grieved at their hardness of heart, and said to the man, "Stretch out your hand." He stretched it out, and his hand was restored." (Mark 3:2–5)

He felt indignation, but didn't act out. He simply healed the man's arm. Consider, too, some of the ways Jesus commanded us to act as people of faith. What would be your immediate reaction if I smacked you on the side of the head? And what did Jesus say we're supposed to do when someone smacks us on the side of the head? Most likely you know the answer: turn the other cheek. What would you do if it was a cold day and someone came up to you and held a knife to your throat and said, "Give me your coat"? What did Jesus say we're supposed to do when we are in a situation like that? "Take my sweater too." Where does the ability to respond like that come from? *Apatheia.*

Apatheia and Fear

What about fear? We *know* that Jesus felt fear—in the garden at Gethsemane, right before his crucifixion, he was so overcome with anxiety that the sweat fell from his head like great drops of blood. "Father take this cup from me," he cried (Luke 22:42). Jesus felt the fear, but he didn't allow it to guide his actions. When we see how he passed through his passion—the betrayal, the injustice of the trial, the humiliation, the scourging and mocking, the beating, the crucifixion itself—it is miraculous. He faced the entire thing with *apatheia*, with an inner peace, an inner freedom, an inner trust in God.

Another great New Testament model for *apatheia* is St. Stephen, the first Christian martyr (Acts 7). He was able to face the murderous hostility of a mob with joyous courage even as he was being stoned to death. Fear had no place in his heart. He was free and at peace. We have the similar witness of countless martyrs across history, even right down to the twentieth century, even our own decade—Christians who are able to face even the most fearsome things with complete peace and freedom. Where does that ability come from? *Apatheia*.

Roland Joffe's great 1986 film *The Mission* tells the true story of how a group of Jesuit missionaries entered the Paraguayan Plateau in South America in the 1750s. They won the Guarani people there to faith and created a Christian society of incredible simplicity and beauty. Yet corrupt officials of both church and government demanded that the Jesuits dismantle the community so the indigenous people could be taken as slaves. When the Jesuits refuse, troops are sent in, and the indigenous are no match for their military might. While the Guarani are being overwhelmed with violence, the Jesuit father Gabriel leads a procession from the church, carrying a monstrance aloft. When he is shot down, Guarani children pick up the montrance and carry it to safety in the rainforest. Where does such courage come from? *Apatheia*.

Apatheia and Gluttony

Let's look at desire and the anxiety we feel about having enough. Remember what Jesus said:

> "Therefore I tell you, do not worry about your life, what you will eat or what you will drink, or about your body, what you will wear. Is not life more than food, and the body more than clothing? Look at the birds of the air; they neither sow nor reap nor gather into barns, and yet your heavenly Father feeds them. Are you not of more value than they? And can any of you by worrying add a single hour to your span of life? And why do you worry about clothing? Consider the lilies of the field, how they grow; they neither toil nor spin, yet I tell you, even Solomon in all his glory was not clothed like one of these. But if God so clothes the grass of the field, which is alive today and tomorrow is thrown into the oven, will he not

much more clothe you—you of little faith? Therefore do not worry, saying, 'What will we eat?' or 'What will we drink?' or 'What will we wear?' For it is the Gentiles who strive for all these things; and indeed your heavenly Father knows that you need all these things. But strive first for the kingdom of God and his righteousness, and all these things will be given to you as well." (Matt 6:25–33)

First trust in God, and all your needs will be met. Do you believe that? Really? Are you willing to give up this inner drive, this inner imperative, this desire to have, to layer ourselves over with things?

There are Christians who have been able to achieve this. We all know about great saints like Francis of Assisi. But there are contemporary examples. Several years ago I watched a documentary about the Blessed Sisters of Charity.[2] The sisters were opening a new house in San Francisco in order to minister to AIDS victims. The bishop of San Francisco was delighted to have them. He provided a house, which he furnished with all of the finest amenities. Then, on camera, when the nuns arrived and the bishop greeted them and was showing them around, the abbess of the house said, "Take all this furniture out of here." The bishop couldn't understand why. "This is luxurious," she told him. "We sleep on pallets on the floor." The bishop could not wrap his mind around it. He couldn't understand why anyone would choose to live with such simplicity and freedom, without any care for material comforts. This is *apatheia*.

The most free person I ever met was Neil Russell, the Anglican bishop of Zanzibar during the period of colonial revolution in the early 1960s. He was imprisoned for a time, and after his release he went to live at the Community of the Transfiguration in Roslyn, Scotland, outside of Edinburgh. I first became conscious of him when I repeatedly saw his picture in the newspaper—at government events talking with prominent politicians, or at social engagements talking with members of the nobility, or on his knees in the worst slums of Glasgow chatting with little children. I found myself asking, "Who is this man who seems so comfortable with any level of society?"

When I finally met him, I was immediately attracted by his winsome personality. He seemed to be without guile—open and vulnerable, always ready to laugh. One day, he invited me to have lunch with him at the monastery. Believe me, by any epicurean standard, this was one of the worst meals I ever encountered. It consisted of watery potato soup and very rough bread, not at all tasty. Then he took me to see where he lived. It was

---

2. Muggeridge, *Vintage Muggeridge*, 42.

an unheated little shack, which he called his "cell." He opened the door to the single room. It held a bed, a small table with a straight-backed chair, a small chest of drawers, and a crucifix on the wall. That was it. All the clothing he owned was either on his back, in that little dresser, or hanging on a hook behind the door. He was a man completely, utterly unshackled by greed. Possessions did not hinder him. He was able to go anyplace in society, totally unencumbered by greed. He was utterly free.

The Gift of *Apatheia*

I am positive that God doesn't want many of us to become an apostle or a prophet or a martyr or even a monk or nun. But I am also sure that it is God's desire for every one of us to experience the reality of *apatheia*. Are you ever subject to anger, fear, gluttony, or greed? Do these emotions cause you and others pain? Would you like to have inner freedom and peace? Ultimately, the only way to get it is as a radical gift of grace. It cannot be bought; it cannot be learned; it cannot be achieved. But we can receive it simply by becoming conscious of it, and asking God for it.

    I don't think one out of a thousand people in America have even heard of *apatheia*. But to simply know that it exists—that it is part of the reality of the Christian life—opens us to its grace. I pray for the gift of *apatheia* every day. When I become aware of anger or fear or desire welling up within me, in that moment, I try to be conscious enough to ask God for this gift.

    "Muscle memory" is the idea that if you practice your golf swing or your tennis backhand long enough, pretty soon your muscles are essentially programmed to do it. Your muscles remember, and just take over. There is also a concept called "spiritual memory." As we offer ourselves to God and we become disciplined to pray for certain things, we respond to our circumstances in particular ways. If we focus on *apatheia*, we will find that when we feel negative things welling up inside us, we won't give in, but instead will find ourselves asking God to bless us with this inner freedom and peace.

    As a gift of grace, *apatheia* is not something that is my or anyone else's possession. But when I pray for it, day in and day out, week in and week out, there are moments of grace. I feel peace, yes. I feel an inner freedom, yes. But that is not why God gives this gift. God gives us peace and freedom so that we may become redemptive witnesses to those around us. That is why the desert fathers so prized *apatheia*. That's why a real Christian life begins with *apatheia*, because this virtue sets us free to witness to the gospel. When we receive *apatheia*, we are set free to be fully part of the body of Christ. *Apatheia* is the gift of God that enables us to become the people God created us to be.

Chapter 6

Peace

> *Peace I leave with you; my peace I give to you; not as the world gives do I give to you. Let not your hearts be troubled, neither let them be afraid.* (John 14:27)

IF YOU COULD HAVE any wish fulfilled, what would you ask for? Context matters here. If you were sick, you might wish for health. If you were in a financial pinch, you might desire money. If someone you love has hurt you, you might seek reconciliation, or revenge, or both. If you're feeling overwhelmed by the demands of your life, you might hope for rest, for a holiday. If you or someone you love is facing death, you might ask for prolonged life.

Now let me put the question differently, as a person of faith. Do you think that what God wants for you may be different from what you want for yourself? If God were to give you any gift—right now, here and now—what do you think *God* would want that to be? Would it be health or money? Reconciliation or revenge or rest? Would it be for prolonged life?

I don't think it would be any of these, and I suspect you don't either. But I do think there is a gift that God does want for each of us, one that is precious regardless of our circumstances. It is a gift that is of inestimable value under any circumstances.

It is peace. It is the first thing Jesus bestowed upon his followers after his resurrection. As stated above in the Gospel of John, Jesus declares, "Peace I leave with you; not as the world gives; but my peace I leave with you."[1]

---

1. Author's paraphrase.

God's Gift of Peace

How precious a gift is this? So precious, it is the thing St. Paul wants for Christians more than anything else. He says it in every letter he wrote in the New Testament, "Grace to you and peace from God our Father and the Lord Jesus Christ." He says it to the Romans, the Corinthians twice, the Philippians, the Galatians, the Colossians, the Thessalonians twice, to Timothy twice, to Titus, and to Philemon. For St. Paul, peace may be the most precious of all God's gifts.

If that surprises you, it's important to remember exactly what Jesus said to his disciples: "My peace I leave with you." It is not the world's peace; the world's peace is just temporary, but God's peace is very different. We tend to think about peace as the end of something bad. When people are shooting at one another, peace is what we call a "ceasefire." If we are in physical pain when we're sick, or emotional pain when someone has hurt us, peace is when the pain stops. If we suffer anxiety when money is short or when there's just too much to do, peace is that financial windfall or that week off. If we anguish over the prospect of our own death, or the death of a loved one, peace is when there is a reprieve and death goes into temporary retreat. But that's just it—all of these moments of peace are moments; they are only temporary. We will be sick again. People will hurt us again. We will worry about money again. We will be driven to distraction again. And we will, every one of us, die.

But God's peace—the peace Jesus gave to his disciples, the peace Paul wanted for all Christians—is different. It is not just the end, the cessation, a reprieve from suffering. No, God's peace is rooted in the Hebrew concept of *shalom*: a positive sense of well-being that doesn't depend on circumstances, but flows out from the human heart, blessing every aspect of our lives. Jesus and Paul took this notion even further. The Greek word for peace in the New Testament is *irene*, which has passed into English as the female name Irene. It describes a pervasive well-being that is found only in relationship with God. Far from being temporary, it lasts forever. As Jesus said, "Those who love me will keep my word, and my Father will love them, and we will come and make our home with them" (John 14:23). What we will then know is peace.

Peace When Confronted with Violence

One of the most iconic stories in the Hebrew Bible is that of David and Goliath. Over the centuries it has so impressed itself on Western consciousness, it has become our primary metaphor for the struggle of the weak against the strong. I remember walking down the street in Manhattan in the fall of 2007 and passing a newsstand, seeing a huge, bold banner headline reading, "DAVID BEATS GOLIATH." Well, I had to buy the paper. It recounted perhaps the greatest upset in college football history: Appalachian State 34 – Michigan 32. When in 2013 Malcolm Gladwell published a bestselling book called *David and Goliath: Underdogs, Misfits and the Art of Battling Giants*, no one had to ask who David and Goliath were.

But whenever I read about the actual confrontation in 1 Samuel 17, I am deeply struck, but not by the mere fact of David defeating the giant Philistine who had terrorized Israel's entire army. No, what moves me is David's affect. He is facing brutal violence that is likely to end in his death. Yet in God's grace he is completely at peace.

> The Philistine said to David, "Come to me, and I will give your flesh to the birds of the air and to the wild animals of the field." But David said to the Philistine, "You come to me with sword and spear and javelin; but I come to you in the name of the LORD of hosts, the God of the armies of Israel, whom you have defied. This very day the Lord will deliver you into my hand . . ." (vv. 44–46a)

"I come to you in the name of the Lord of hosts . . ." David still had to face Goliath, but he was unafraid. In grace he had been given the gift of God's peace.

Mel Gibson's 2016 film *Hacksaw Ridge* tells the true story of Desmond Doss, a conscientious objector during World War II. Although he enlisted in the military as a medic, Doss (played by Andrew Garfield) refused to carry a weapon because of his Christian belief: "Thou shall not kill."[2] In the Battle of Okinawa, his unit is ordered to take a tall escarpment they nicknamed Hacksaw Ridge from the Japanese army. The fighting is fierce and many of Doss's comrades lie wounded on the field of battle, crying out for help. Doss alone returns to save them, as he says in the film, "Everyone else is taking life. I'm going to be saving it." He carries each man to the cliff's edge, then lowers each down by rope before returning to save another. The survival of dozens of soldiers who were thought dead is a shock

---

2. Mel Gibson, dir., *Hacksaw Ridge* (2016).

to the American soldiers below. Doss himself is shot, but still seeks out the wounded until the battle is over. He was later awarded the Congressional Medal of Honor. What enabled him to carry on in the chaos and violence of battle until every wounded man was saved? The gift of God's peace.

Peace in the Midst of Pain

It is interesting to me that perhaps the single Christian in history who suffered the most pain for the sake of the gospel is none other than he who wrote about half of the New Testament. Yes, I mean the apostle Paul. In his Second Letter to the Corinthians, he lists some of the pain he had endured:

> Five times I have received from the Jews the forty lashes minus one. Three times I was beaten with rods. Once I received a stoning. Three times I was shipwrecked; for a night and a day I was adrift at sea; on frequent journeys, in danger from rivers, danger from bandits, danger from my own people, danger from Gentiles, danger in the city, danger in the wilderness, danger at sea, danger from false brothers and sisters; in toil and hardship, through many a sleepless night, hungry and thirsty, often without food, cold and naked. (2 Cor 11:23–27)

And he didn't even mention the time he was kidnapped (Acts 21:27), his multiple arrests and imprisonments (Acts 21:23; 22:24–31; 23:35; 28:16), let alone being bitten by a poisonous snake (Acts 28:3). His life ended with his execution in Rome.

Paul, not surprisingly, had bad moments. As he wrote to the Corinthians,

> We do not want you to be unaware, brothers and sisters, of the affliction we experienced in Asia; for we were so utterly, unbearably crushed that we despaired of life itself. (2 Cor 1:8)

But Paul also understood the peace that came through faith in Jesus Christ. That's why he opened each of his letters in the New Testament by asking God to bestow peace on everyone who read those letters. In his own life, Paul experienced God's peace in the midst of his tribulations, so he could write, "We know that all things work together for good for those who love God, who are called according to his purpose" (Rom 8:28). Paul goes on:

> Who will separate us from the love of Christ? Will hardship, or distress, or persecution, or famine, or nakedness, or peril, or sword?

As it is written, "For your sake we are being killed all day long; we are accounted as sheep to be slaughtered." No, in all these things we are more than conquerors through him who loved us. For I am convinced that neither death, nor life, nor angels, nor rulers, nor things present, nor things to come, nor powers, nor height, nor depth, nor anything else in all creation, will be able to separate us from the love of God in Christ Jesus our Lord. (Rom 8:35–39)

I once had a harrowing conversation with a young couple who came to me for premarital counseling. Several months before, they had gone to an exhibit at an art museum when—out of nowhere—she was suddenly assaulted by a series of hallucinations. At first, strolling through the galleries, she was able to separate herself from them, even telling her fiancé that she was hallucinating. But after a few minutes she was completely overcome by loathsome, dreadful visions. Completely out of her mind, she was taken to a nearby hospital, where she had to be strapped down to prevent her from hurting herself and others.

For days, the doctors didn't know what was wrong with her, and struggled to find a treatment that helped. She would have short periods of lucidity, only to be overwhelmed again by the horror. Finally, the doctors diagnosed encephalitis, a viral infection of the brain. Although they could treat the underlying symptoms with antibiotics and steroids, encephalitis itself was caused by a virus. Like any other virus, they could only let it run its course. In those fleeting periods of clarity, the young woman felt not only that God had abandoned her, but that God had cast her into hell.

But during one of her lucid moments, she prayed. And when the prayer ended, she turned to her fiancé and with a gentle laugh told him, "Don't worry. I'm going to be alright." Later that day she slipped into a coma; the doctors told her parents and fiancé that it was possible she would die. The young man said, "No, she's going to recover. I know it." He had surprised even himself. He didn't know why he knew; he just knew. After days of dread, he was filled with certainty and peace.

She didn't die. She came out of the coma and recovered very quickly. Later, describing the experience to me, she said that despite feeling utterly forsaken by God, in reality God had been with her in every moment. She told me that in her weakness—in the heart of her helplessness—she met God in Jesus Christ. He brought her a peace that knows no bounds. She now knew that what Paul wrote to the Corinthians is true: that God is faithful and will never let us be tested beyond our strength.

Peace When Confronting Death

What is it that keeps us from knowing this peace? From the time I was a little boy—as long as I can remember—I have suffered from a particular malady where, just as I drift off to sleep, I would be hit with a sense of overwhelming dread and shake myself awake. Have you ever had an experience like that? Sometimes this pattern became so burdensome that I would spend the day worrying about not being able to fall asleep later that night. Only as a young adult, with the help of a psychotherapist, did I come to realize that this was caused by a fear of losing control, and ultimately a fear of death. Who knew what might happen if I let myself slip into oblivion? I might not ever come back. I might never wake again. I might be trapped in a demon-dominated hell. As Hamlet mused, "To die? Perchance to dream? Ay there's the rub."[3] Aye there's the rub. Who knew what nightmares awaited me out there where I had absolutely no control?

In the autumn of 1977, my former wife and I were living in Edinburgh, Scotland. Our parents were living in Hawaii. One day we received a call from her father, who told us that her mother had some abdominal swelling and they were going to perform exploratory surgery. This was long before MRIs and CAT scans existed. My father-in-law was a physician, and he said he wasn't very worried, but simply wanted to keep us informed. He called back the next day to say that during the surgery they discovered she was full of cancer, so metastasized that there was nothing they could do. He thought she only had about three weeks to live, and he asked us to come to Hawaii and be with them.

Our firstborn, David, was only four months old, and the trip was excruciating. But we managed to get to Maui in just a few days. My mother-in-law had been brought home, and her condition deteriorated very quickly. The next couple of weeks were among the most stressful I've ever experienced. She spent more and more time either unconscious or hallucinating, and moments of lucidity became rare. I had never really considered her to be a person of strong faith, but in one of her periods of clarity the two of us fell into a long conversation about life after death. I was astounded by the simplicity and purity of her belief.

She eventually went into a coma and her breathing became labored. You could hear it rattling from all over the house. One evening my father-in-law called us into her room and said the end was near. There were six

---

3. Shakespeare, *Hamlet*, act 3, scene 1.

of us: my former wife, her father, her sister and brother-in-law, her godmother, and me. We stood around my mother-in-law's bed, held hands, and prayed. Just before she died, the quality of light in the room changed. Everyone noticed it. At the very moment of her death, the Lord Jesus Christ was in the room with us. I saw, I felt, I heard, I experienced him taking my mother-in-law into his arms.

That event changed me forever. From that moment I have no longer been afraid of death. I looked death in the face and saw that Jesus Christ is there. As he said to his disciples, "You heard me say to you, I am going away, and I am coming to you. Those who love me will keep my word, and my Father will love them, and we will come to them and make our home with them" (John 14:23). Now, when I am just about to fall asleep, just about to slip into the darkness, and I feel the dread and desire to shake myself awake, I laugh out loud. For I know even when I look into the abyss, Jesus is there.

That is God's peace. It is not the temporary cessation of pain, but a state of profound well-being found in relationship with God, and it lasts forever. It is ours even in the midst of sickness and rejection, even in the midst of stress and worry. It reaches even beyond death. It is the most precious gift we can receive.

What I've described above is an inner reality known only by faith. For Christians, the inner cacophony of our desires and fears are silenced, our envy and greed stilled. It is in this quiet that we stand in the presence of God. And in that peace, we begin to understand and know the spiritual blessings of God's kingdom made manifest, made real to us by an inner knowledge and experience of God's love, joy, and hope. But that's only the first part in understanding the virtuous nature of peace.

Carrying Peace into the World

Even though experiencing God is an inner reality, in our hearts and minds, we are also called to go out into the world bearing witness to God's truth. We are to uphold godly values of justice and equality not only in our own lives, but in our community, in American society, and on into the rest of the world. Ralph Waldo Emerson wrote that "the only reward of virtue is virtue,"[4] but Christian virtues are not ends in themselves. To be Christian means to look beyond ourselves and recognize we have a role in the world as well. I have always tried to challenge my congregations to manifest these

---

4. Emerson, *Friendship*, 33.

values through multiple ministries, both locally and abroad. This outreach has included addressing homelessness, hunger, and discrimination at home, and as far away as Bolivia, Liberia, Ecuador, Honduras, and South Africa. One of my parishes had nearly one thousand members engaged in regular ministry. Why? In the hope of bringing the peace of God to at least some people in those places.

As Jesus said in Matthew 25, this is the peace of God that takes root when prisoners are visited, the hungry are fed, the thirsty receive drink, the naked are clothed, the sick are cared for, and the stranger is welcomed. When those things are accomplished—when that outer peace is established—the poor can hear the good news. It is through outreach that we bear witness to the values of the kingdom of God; it gives us credibility when we're given the opportunity to share the inner values of God's love, joy, hope, and peace. As Jesus said, "Blessed are the peacemakers, for they shall be called the children of God" (Matt 5:9).

Of course, we now live in a society rent with strife. In the maelstrom of social discourse pitting right against left, conservative against liberal, red against blue, where are the Christian voices? Many trumpet that the United States is a Christian nation, but where is the evidence of that? Historically, the United States has reflected only a patina of Christian values. Take racism as a single example. As Christians we are called to bear witness against it and work for racial healing, yet systemic racism has poisoned our national character. That's not all. Despite a biblical imperative to welcome the stranger, the US government has ripped apart families on our borders. We are the wealthiest nation in history, yet millions of our own people don't have adequate medical care and millions of our children struggle with hunger. Where are the Christian voices calling our politicians and government officials to accountability for feeding the hungry, clothing the naked, healing the sick, and welcoming the stranger? Would you like to live in a nation where God's peace reigned? Can there ever be peace until those issues are adequately addressed for everyone?

Seeking God's Gifts

So, if you could receive any gift from God, here and now, what would it be? Peace, perhaps, both inner and outer? Remember, God's peace is not the temporary cessation of pain. It is a peace that lasts forever, even in the midst of sickness and rejection. That peace is ours even in the midst of stress and worry. That peace reaches even beyond death. But God's peace is not an end in itself. It is given to us so that we may become agents of redemption in the world—true peacemakers. As Jesus said, "Peace I leave with you; not as the world gives, my peace I give to you" (John 14:27).

But how do we move into peace? Ultimately it turns on forgiveness. Many of us struggle with an insistent inner voice that something is wrong with us. As long as it's in play, we cannot know peace. For many of us, that voice telling us we're not okay belongs to our parents. For me, it was my father's voice. He was a congregational minister, very successful and beloved in his community. As a child, I equated my father with God. And since I perceived my father as a stern moralist who could do only good, and I saw myself as someone who did a lot that was bad, I spent much of my childhood and adolescence hiding, keeping secret who I really was. I was sure if my father truly knew me, he would scorn and reject me. And if my father was like that, I assumed God must be like that as well.

When I came to Christian faith—when I had my life shattered and reborn by a mystical encounter with the risen Lord Jesus Christ—I knew in the core of my being that God loved and accepted me. Psychologically, this realization led to anger and resentment when I clearly saw that God wasn't anything at all like my distant, disapproving father. This wasn't really my father's fault, but it still tied me up inside that I never felt I had won his approval. I also discovered that I could not enter into the fullness of God's peace until I was able to forgive my father. Forgiving him became the key to my really understanding God's forgiveness and the nature of the Christian life.

In his great book *After Virtue*, Alisdair MacIntyre writes about this spiritual reality:

> Forgiveness requires that the offender already accepts as just the verdict of the law upon his action and behaves as one who acknowledges the justice of the appropriate punishment; hence the common root of 'penance' and of 'punishment'. The offender can then be forgiven, if the person offended against so wills. That practice of forgiveness presupposes the practices of justice, but there is a crucial difference. Justice is characteristically administered by a judge, an impersonal authority representing the whole community; but forgiveness can only be extended by the offended party. The virtue exhibited in forgiveness is charity (agape). There is no

words in the Greek of Aristotle's age correctly translated 'sin,' 'repentance,' or 'charity.'[5]

There are two steps to receiving God's peace. The first is to recognize that the peace of God that destroys anger and envy will become ours when we consciously enter into the fullness of forgiveness. Secondly, we must recognize that God's peace is not an end in itself, and we may only know it when we commit to be peacemakers in the world.

---

5. MacIntyre, *After Virtue*, 174.

Chapter 7

Kindness

> *By contrast, the fruit of the Spirit is love, joy, peace, patience, kindness, generosity, faithfulness, gentleness, and self-control. There is no law against such things.* (Gal 5:22–23)

I HAVE SPENT YEARS reflecting on godly virtues: reading about them across the arc of Christian spirituality, preaching on them on multiple occasions, and teaching them in literally dozens of classes. I have made lists of these virtues time and again. Yet it is only recently I have come to realize that every list I had done over the years, with multiple additions and subtractions, was missing a key element of Christian character. No account of Christian virtue can be complete without including kindness and its boon companion gentleness. Although a distinct virtue, gentleness is in many ways an extension of kindness.

What is so surprising about my blindness to the significance of kindness and gentleness is that they are everywhere in Scripture. In the Hebrew Bible, kindness is in the most iconic verse on how God calls us to live a godly life: "To do justice, to love kindness and to walk humbly with your God" (Mic 6:8). In the New Testament kindness and gentleness are named as godly imperatives over one hundred times, including in all the significant lists of Christian virtue: 2 Corinthians 6:6; Philippians 4:5; Galatians 5:22; 6:1, and 22; Ephesians 4:32; Colossians 3:12; 1 Timothy 6:11; 2 Timothy 2:24–25; and James 3:13. So how exactly are we to think about kindness as a godly virtue?

Kindness Is Not Niceness

Kindness and niceness may look alike from the outside. A kind person and a nice person may treat people in the very same way, but their inner motivation couldn't be more different. The Christian virtue of kindness always wills the good of the other. It is not interested in any self-aggrandizement. Niceness may be the very opposite. A person may be nice in order to manipulate another to get something from them. Years ago, I came home from work one day to discover my next-door neighbor Jim had cut our grass. He was out working in his yard, so I called over the hedge between our properties and thanked him. He waved off my thanks and said, "Just being neighborly." Two days later I answered a knock at our door. It was Jim. With a smile on his face he said. "My wife and I are going out of town for the weekend. Would you mind taking care of our dog?"

There are also people who are nice in order to protect themselves. Sometimes this is the overly nice person who is always sweet, helpful, and complementary so that everyone will like and accept him. But this kind of behavior can also have a darker side. I had a parishioner once named June who was married to a man named Bill. I felt Bill had undiagnosed borderline personality disorder. There were times when he was vibrant and vivacious, charming and witty. At other times he would prowl around his house in a dark, foul mood. His rages could spring out suddenly at any time if he was contradicted, challenged, or didn't get his own way. His rage would smother his wife and children with horrific verbal abuse. June and her children were always on guard, walking on eggshells, being overly nice simply to never provoke him.

Kindness, on the other hand, is never manipulative. It seeks nothing for self, but is only concerned for the other. Which is why in Scripture kindness is often linked with love and compassion, particularly God's love and compassion. It is God's lovingkindness (in Hebrew *chesed*) that protects the faithful, as in Psalm 36:7, "How excellent is your lovingkindness, O God, all people may take refuge under your wings." Lovingkindness is the foundation of God's redemption of sinful humanity, "I will betroth you to Me forever; Yes, I will betroth you to Me in righteousness and in justice, in lovingkindness and in compassion" (Hos 2:19). It was God's kindness that led to the incarnation:

> But when the goodness and lovingkindness of God our Savior appeared, he saved us, not because of any works of righteousness

that we had done, but according to his mercy, through the water of rebirth and renewal by the Holy Spirit. (Titus 3:4–7)

Perhaps there is nothing more precious a human being can experience than the lovingkindness of God. As the psalmist declared, "Because your lovingkindness is better than life, my lips will praise you" (Ps 63:3).

A nice person also has no concern for the truth, often telling flattering lies in order to manipulate or control others. Kindness is a champion of the truth. My wife Darlene says the kindest thing you can do is tell someone the truth, but with gentleness. That is even the rule when we are in position to bear witness to our faith. As the apostle Peter wrote in his first letter,

> Always be ready to make your defense to anyone who demands from you an account of the hope that is in you; yet do it with gentleness and reverence. (1 Pet 3:15a–16b)

Kindness Upholds Goodness and Justice with Compassion.

When encountering injustice, niceness is often weak, overlooking and even ignoring evil. Kindness is never weak. When faced with injustice, it is fierce, passionate, and strong. In the Gospel story of the woman taken in adultery, Jesus shows the strength of kindness.

> Early in the morning he came again to the temple. All the people came to him and he sat down and began to teach them. The scribes and the Pharisees brought a woman who had been caught in adultery; and making her stand before all of them, they said to him, "Teacher, this woman was caught in the very act of committing adultery. Now in the law Moses commanded us to stone such women. Now what do you say?" They said this to test him, so that they might have some charge to bring against him. Jesus bent down and wrote with his finger on the ground. When they kept on questioning him, he straightened up and said to them, "Let anyone among you who is without sin be the first to throw a stone at her." And once again he bent down and wrote on the ground. When they heard it, they went away, one by one, beginning with the elders; and Jesus was left alone with the woman standing before him. Jesus straightened up and said to her, "Woman, where are they? Has no one condemned you?" She said, "No one, sir." And Jesus said, "Neither do I condemn you. Go your way, and from now on do not sin again." (John 8:2–11)

The scribes and Pharisees had only malice for both the woman and Jesus. Jesus silently addressed the injustice of the situation; after all, it takes two to commit adultery. Where was the adulterous man? Why wasn't he publicly humiliated as well? Writing in the dust, perhaps a list of sins, Jesus challenged the cruel leaders of Jerusalem by asking, "Let anyone among you who is without sin be the first to throw a stone at her." After each slinked off, he addressed the woman. He didn't overlook her sin, but was kind. "Neither do I condemn you. Go your way, and from now on do not sin again."

In J. R. R. Tolkien's *The Lord of the Rings* Bilbo Baggins comes into the possession of the Ring of Power, which holds the fate of all civilization. Bilbo's nephew Frodo is given the fearsome task of destroying the Ring of Power in order to save all goodness in the world. Frodo becomes aware he is being stalked by the vicious, murderous creature Gollum, who wants the ring for himself. In discussion with his mentor, the wizard Gandolf, Frodo says, "What a pity that Bilbo didn't stab that vile creature, when he had a chance!" Gandolf replies, "Pity. It was pity that stayed his hand. Pity, and Mercy: not to strike without need. . . My heart tells me that he has some part to play yet, for good or ill, before the end; and when that comes the pity of Bilbo may rule the fate of many—yours not the least."[1] When later in the tale Frodo and his companion Samwise Gamgee capture Gollum, Sam wants to kill him. Frodo chooses mercy, and with firm kindness allows Gollum to guide them to Mordor. Ultimately the ring is destroyed, because with great wisdom and strength both Bilbo and Frodo chose kindness.

In Victor Hugo's *Les Miserables*, Jean Valjean is doomed to a life of misery and degradation. Released after serving nearly twenty years in prison with nowhere to go, he is invited into the home of a bishop. Valjean responds to the bishop's hospitality by stealing his valuable silver candlesticks. The police quickly capture him and return him to the bishop. He is facing more decades of misery in prison. But . . . the bishop tells the police he gave the silver to Valjean as a gift. He chose mercy over vengeance. His act of kindness did not overlook Valjean's crime. The bishop chose to forgive, but he tells Valjean,

> Jean Valjean, my brother. You no longer belong to evil. With this silver I bought your soul. I have ransomed you from fear and hatred. And now I give you back to God.[2]

---

1. Tolkien *Fellowship*, 77.
2. Hugo, *Les Miserables*, 372.

Valjean, given a new start by the kindness of the bishop, lived the rest of his life fighting injustice and helping those in need. He even forgave his own mortal enemy, Inspector Javert.

Kindness Changes Us

Niceness not only ignores injustice; it also costs nothing. For many, being nice is a type of emotional armor to hide behind. There is a cost to kindness, both spiritually and emotionally. Kindness demands that we be vulnerable to others, because a kind person is always empathetic. Our acts of kindness certainly will bless the recipients of them, but they will also change us. Barry Corey writes that kindness makes us receivable, open to change.

> My own instincts are to live in a way that implies to others that I have my future plotted and my life just right. The way of kindness removes, or at least lowers, the mask. It's not necessarily a life of transparency, which means everything can be seen. But it is at least a life of translucency, where we let light shine through ourselves that reveals the messiness in which we all journey.[3]

Sometimes simply witnessing the kindness of someone else helps us see our own messiness and change how we ourselves will act in the future. Several years ago on a trip to Kansas City, I met a man named Jack who was running a ministry for the homeless. It emerged during our conversation that Jack had a law degree from an Ivy League school and had once been a partner in a prestigious law firm. When I asked why he had given up the law for ministry, he responded by saying it had begun when he was on a business trip to New York City. It was winter, and like so many other visitors he was appalled at the numbers of homeless, derelict people who were living on the streets. One evening when he was riding the subway, his thoughts on the subject became focused when he noticed a homeless woman curled up asleep on a seat opposite him. The temperature outside was below freezing and she was wearing only a light jacket. Her hands were red and chapped.

Jack prided himself on his Christian faith and commitment to ministry. Although he was saddened and sympathetic about the sleeping woman, he was at a loss as to what he could actually do for her. But soon thoughts began to enter Jack's mind that distanced him from the situation. There

---

3. Corey, *Love Kindness*, 31.

really was nothing he could do. The problem of homelessness was so immense. Why wasn't the Salvation Army more active? And what about the city government? It's ultimately their responsibility. What do people pay taxes for anyway? In his ire, his blame of others, his righteous indignation, he forgot completely about the homeless woman. Just then the train pulled into a station. Jack noticed a young Hispanic man move toward the open door. Before leaving the train, he paused to stand over the sleeping homeless woman. Just before the doors snapped shut and he stepped off the train, the young man dropped a pair of warm winter gloves—the gloves he had been wearing—on the body of the sleeping woman.

Jack said it was like a sharp slap across his face. It shattered the illusion that he was a big-deal Christian. He heard the voice of Jesus ringing in his mind: "If you have done it to the least of these my brethren, you have done it unto me" (Matt 25:40). Jack told me he couldn't get that act of kindness out of his mind. It eventually led him to change his vocation, so he could show kindness to the homeless all the time. Simply witnessing the kindness of another can transform us.

I understood what Jack had experienced. When I lived in New York City, I took pride in being "street smart." This is the ability to sense when something is not right while walking down the street, and thus taking appropriate action to avoid trouble. One day years ago, when I was serving at Grace Church, I took an elderly parishioner out to lunch. We both had appointments back at the church's parish house at 1:00 o'clock, so after lunch we were hurrying to be back on time. When we got to 10th and Broadway, and I looked across the street, there was a man standing right in front of the church who made me feel uneasy. He was dirty and disheveled, but that was normal for the homeless in New York. No, it was something more, something menacing. So instead of crossing the street on that corner, I steered my elderly companion up the west side of Broadway to 11th Street, crossed there, and walked down to the parish house. When we got closer to him, the man suddenly began shouting obscenities, and accosting passersby in a deranged manner. As I deftly guided my older friend into the parish house, completely avoiding any confrontation with the man, I silently congratulated myself on my street smarts.

Then, after all that, my appointment was late. It was with my late friend B. J. Weber, so I shouldn't have been surprised. B. J. was a person who was unacquainted with punctuality. As I waited in my office . . . 1:15 . . . 1:30 . . . 1:45 . . . I got more and more irritated. I couldn't wait until B. J. got there, because I was really going to bust his chops. Finally, at 2:30 B. J. breezed into my office. Before I could launch into my tirade, he said, "Did you see that crazy guy in front of your church?" I thought for a second before responding, "Yeah?" "Well," B. J. said, "it took me awhile, but I finally talked him into going into alcohol rehab. I walked him over to the Bowery Mission and got him enrolled in their program."

As I sat there, completely deflated, all I could think about were the words of Jesus: "You shall love the Lord your God with all your heart, and with all your soul, and with all your mind." This is the greatest and first commandment. And a second is like it: "You shall love your neighbor as yourself" (Matt 22:37–39). Love our neighbor. Who is our neighbor? Could he or she be anyone who is hungry or thirsty? Anyone who is in prison? Anyone who is lonely? Anyone without a home? Anyone without a green card? Could our neighbor be any human being in need? The truth is street smarts have little cache in the kingdom of God. That event took place forty years ago, and ever since almost every time I see a homeless person, I am reminded of B. J.'s kindness that day, and how God wants all of us to live like that.

Kindness May Lead Us into the Very Heart of God

My friend Jack Gilpin argues there is also a further step, where empathy so opens us to others, it is almost as if the kind person assumes the other's nature. Is there a link between this understanding of kindness and God's plan of salvation? Is God's kindness so an extension of God's *agape*, it is what led to the incarnation? As St. Paul wrote to the Galatians,

> Let the same mind be in you that was in Christ Jesus, who, though he was in the form of God, did not regard equality with God as something to be exploited, but emptied himself, taking the form of a slave, being born in human likeness. And being found in human form, he humbled himself and became obedient to the point of death—even death on a cross. (Gal 2:5–8)

The inference of this passage (called the "Carmen Christi") is that the kindness of God led to both the incarnation and the atonement. God the Son's empathy for humanity was so great, he emptied himself of divinity and became human. Why? In order to redeem us on the cross. St. Paul was even more focused on this when he wrote to the Romans that God's kindness undergirds our own repentance and salvation: "Or do you presume upon the riches of his kindness and forbearance and patience? Do you not know that God's kindness is meant to lead you to repentance?" (Rom 4:2).

The Christian novelist Charles Williams (1886–1945) described this as "co-inherence."[4] This is actually an ancient theological notion articulated by the early church fathers in their attempts to understand the Trinity. The Greek word *perichoresis* was translated into English as "co-inherence." The three persons of the Trinity not only shared the same essence; they "indwelled" one another. As Jesus declared, their intimacy was so complete, he could say, "I am in the Father and the Father is in me" (John 14:11). Not only that; the salvation he offered could be understood as calling his followers into the same intimacy, "You will know that I am in my Father, and you in me, and I in you" (John 14:20). And Paul extended this cooinherence to the whole church: "so we, who are many, are one body in Christ, and individually we are members one of another" (Rom 12:5).

For Williams co-inherence takes place when one person in the body of Christ takes on another's sorrow or suffering in prayer, "dying in each other's life, living in each other's death."[5] So Christian salvation can never be a solitary affair. Before his death, he intended to found a lay religious order, to be called the Companions of the Co-Inherence, in which its members would practice the kindness of bearing one another's burdens, willing to sacrifice and forgive, living for one another as members of the body of Christ.

Could the World Use More Kindness?

Kindness seems to have fled from American society. Certainly this is true on our roadways, where aggression and rage are now commonplace. Even more telling is the ranting behavior of our political leaders in the public square. The rudeness and bullying behavior in our legislatures and courts is pitiful to behold. How many thoughtful political leaders have abandoned public service because such behavior is now not rare but the rule? Even Christian leaders have been infected, often reacting to the challenges of others with frenzied harshness. As Barry Corey has written, "Our increasingly shrill sounds in the public square, our mean-spirited culture, are not strengthening our witness but weakening it."[6] What would our world be like if there was simply more kindness?

4. Newman, "Charles Williams," 1–26.
5. Williams, *He Came Down from Heaven*, 83.
6. Corey, *Love Kindness*, xix.

Chapter 8

Generosity

> *Give, and it will be given to you. A good measure, pressed down, shaken together, running over, will be put into your lap; for the measure you give will be the measure you get back.* (Luke 6:38)

The Power of Money

MANY YEARS AGO, WHEN I was in ministry at Grace Church in New York, I was in a fellowship group that included a man who was new to faith. One summer, he seemed to go from crisis to crisis. Some concerned his relationships, some concerned his health, but the most pressing were financial. He had lost his job, was heavily in debt, and didn't know where to turn. He was desperate. One day, another man in the fellowship group went to see him. The previous night, he had been rummaging in the back of a desk drawer and discovered a fully mature government bond worth $5,000. "I don't need this," he thought to himself. "I've been quite happy not even knowing it was there. I'll be quite happy without it." So he signed it over to the man who was in crisis. Not ten cents on the dollar, but the whole thing.

Could you have done that? If I found $5,000, I'm not sure if I could. The gesture so impressed me that I made a special effort to talk with the man about his generosity. He was embarrassed that I even knew about it but he finally shared that he gave away one-third of his income every month. He took it off the top—his first priority, month in and month out, was to give away that amount of money. Only then did he work out his own budget. That way, he told me, he never missed the money that might benefit those in real need. When asked about the motivation for his generosity, he laughed and began to tell me a story. He had grown up in Southern Illinois during the Great Depression. His father was a coal miner who labored underground six days a week, and was thankful simply to have a job. Every Saturday evening he would receive his weekly wages: three ten-dollar bills. And, as my friend told me, the next morning he would watch his father put one of those bills into the offering plate at their church. The family was poor, but as my friend said, they never wanted for anything. They had learned they could trust God for their well-being.

As Christians we are called to acknowledge the power money has over us, so that we can manage our finances in a responsible way. How important is this? We have plenty of evidence that there was perhaps nothing more important to Jesus. As a matter of fact, fully 20 percent, one-fifth, of Jesus' teaching in the Synoptic Gospels (Matthew, Mark, and Luke) is about money and stewardship. His first concern about money is that it can enslave us. Often this enslavement is unconscious, so that we don't even think about it. Consequently we fail to recognize, yet alone acknowledge, our greed, or the envy that drives us. Jesus asks us to make a choice. We are called by Jesus to renounce greed and envy. As the Gospel of Matthew teaches:

> No one can serve two masters, for a slave will either hate the one and love the other or be devoted to the one and despise the other. You cannot serve God and wealth. (Matt 6:24)

The Letter of James is even fiercer, reminding us that those who worship money—those who accumulate wealth and ignore the needs of others—will be accountable to God:

> Now listen, you rich people, weep and wail because of the misery that is coming upon you. Your wealth has rotted, and moths have eaten your clothes. Your gold and silver are corroded. Their corrosion will testify against you and eat your flesh like fire. You have hoarded wealth in the last days. Look! The wages you failed to pay the workmen who mowed your fields are crying out against you. The cries of the harvesters have reached the ears of the Lord Almighty. You have lived on earth in luxury and self-indulgence. You have fattened yourselves in the day of slaughter. You have condemned and murdered innocent men, who were not opposing you. (Jas 5:1–6)

The Imperative to Give

Jesus could not be clearer: "It is easier for a camel to go through the eye of a needle than for someone who is rich to enter the kingdom of God" (Matt 10:25) However, Jesus doesn't condemn wealth. He condemns greed and envy. The primary aspect of his teaching about wealth turns on how we are called to share our blessings with others: generously, not as a religious duty, but as the source of profound human joy. The happiest people—those most contented, with the deepest sense of well-being and peace—are the ones who can give away what they have freely, out of a sense of thanksgiving and grace. Do you believe that?

As Christians we are called to dethrone money as a power in our lives. Do you know what cuts the power right of money? Giving it away. Those who freely give money away are liberated from the power it has over us. Show me a truly generous person, and I'll show you someone who is not only happy, but totally free from the power of greed and envy.

As to how much we should give, the biblical standard is the tithe: giving 10 percent of what we have for the work of God—as a minimum. If you manage to reach that level of giving, you are remarkable. In the United States, even self-proclaimed Christians give away less than 4 percent of their income. What does that say about us as a people of faith in response to the will of God?

We all have basic financial needs, obviously, but unlike the vast majority of people on our planet, most Westerners have more than they need to live comfortably. I don't mean luxuriously—comfortably. It is in how we choose to spend that determines whether or not we are being good stewards. After our basic needs are met, we can spend our extra money in four ways. First, we can insulate ourselves with security—buying insurance, investing in real estate, purchasing stocks and bonds. Second, we can accumulate the trappings of luxury, both for ourselves and for those we love. Perhaps you don't feel you live luxuriously, but ask yourself this: how many pairs of shoes do you own? How many do you truly need? Third, we can spend discretionary money on recreation—on sports, on travel, on restaurants, on boats, on second homes, on clubs, on going to the movies.

Or, finally, we can give away our discretionary income for the work of God. Four things: security, luxury, recreation, and charity. Now all of these are appropriate uses of one's resources. But, it seems to me, a good steward will give away at least as much as he or she spends on luxury and recreation. What do you think? How are you doing personally?

Why Is Generosity So Difficult?

Have you ever been poor? Have you ever *felt* that you were poor? When I finished seminary in 1976, I moved to Scotland to begin a PhD program. During the three years my wife and I were there, we lived almost entirely off our savings, which was roughly $20,000. That meant a little less than $7,000 a year, for everything: rent, food, clothing, tuition, tithing, travel, and the birth of two children. Yet we didn't feel poor. One reason was we had lower expectations. Another reason was that nearly everyone with whom we were friendly was living at about the same standard.

After receiving my doctorate in 1979, I accepted a job at St. Bartholomew's Church in New York City. St. Bart's was at 50th Street and Park Avenue, the heart of Midtown Manhattan, on some of the most valuable real estate in the world. My salary was $15,000 a year. That first year my young family lived in the suburbs, where we were house-sitting for my brother, who had temporarily relocated to Switzerland. I tell you, I had never felt so flush, like a king. After we'd been at the church for a few months, a parishioner invited us to spend the weekend with his family in their Park Avenue apartment. He had just become the youngest partner at Goldman Sachs, and his career was soaring. That Friday night, he and I were sent to get diapers for our infant daughters. As the two of us walked down Lexington Avenue, through crowded sidewalks, he put his arm around my shoulder and said, "You know Ken, in New York, if you make less than a hundred grand a year, you're lower middle class."

And that was over forty years ago! Today the number would be closer to half a million. Are you rich? If you don't think so, why is that? Are you able to recognize the insidious power of greed and envy? Feelings of greed and envy can lead even those most financially comfortable to feel that they are poor, that they need more. That's the power money has in our lives—it creates the illusion that we need to protect what we have, and then accumulate even more.

The only thing that will set us free is to give abundantly. The teaching of Jesus is so clear and simple. If we are truly people of faith, we cannot serve both God and money. We are called to make a choice. Where is your loyalty?

The Wrong Reasons for Giving

In reality, godly stewardship is done freely, unconditionally, and for the benefit of others. There are a number of reasons why we give. Some of them are utterly selfish. For example, in the early 1980s I had a friend who was serving on the board of a nonprofit theater group whose mission was to produce plays with a redemptive message. In New York, with fierce theatrical competition, this could be very difficult. Costs were high and, though they felt proud of what they had accomplished, these plays had little chance of commercial success. For a couple of years they barely survived, and going into the third season there was simply not enough money to continue, so to the disappointment of all involved they prepared to shut down. Then, much to everyone's surprise and delight, an "angel" appeared, offering to underwrite the theater's entire budget for the coming year.

But then this "angel" asked for a seat on the board of directors. Then he began dictating who should be hired and fired. He even had the audacity to tell the artistic director what plays to produce, and whom to cast. It turned into a nightmare. Everyone involved became disheartened, ruing the day the "angel" had appeared. He was interested only in power and control, and he eventually destroyed the company. There is nothing godly about that kind of giving.

A similarly misguided motive for giving is the hope of reward. Have you ever received a mailing from a nonprofit that listed the names of contributors? Have you ever eagerly poured over it to see who were the cheapskates that gave only $100, and those who gave over $10,000? Have you ever sat with pen in hand trying to decide whether to give an organization $250 or $500 so that your name could appear as a "patron" rather than as a "donor"? Sometimes the reward is financial. After all, would you be as generous with your donations if there was no tax benefit?

The desire for reward also plays out in large-scale philanthropy. How many major gifts are fueled by the allure of having one's name on a building, or an endowed professorship, or an academic department? Some give away money to launder their reputations. The Sackler family built their fortune with Purdue Pharma, the drug company that developed and relentlessly marketed OxyContin, the opioid that has addicted millions and led to tens of thousands of deaths. While family members assiduously ignore the infamous source of their wealth, the name Sackler appears on wings of major museums in New York, Washington, Boston, and Paris as well as institutes and buildings at Oxford, Columbia, Harvard, and dozens of other universities. As Allen Frances, the former chair of psychiatry at Duke University of Medicine, has said,

> I don't know how many rooms in different parts of the world I've given talks in that were named after the Sacklers. Their name has been pushed forward as the epitome of good works and of the fruits of the capitalist system. But, when it comes down to it, they've earned this fortune at the expense of millions of people who are addicted. It's shocking how they have gotten away with it.[1]

Billy Graham used to tell a story about a time he and his wife Ruth were at church, and when the offering plate was passed, he dropped in a bill. After a few seconds he looked into his wallet and hissed to his wife, "Oh no! I put in a hundred! I only meant to put in a ten." "That's okay, Billy," Ruth replied. "God will only count it as a ten." Godly stewardship is not interested in reward or recognition.

To the shame of the Christian church, many give, sometimes sacrificially, in the hope of a proffered eternal reward. The passion of the Protestant Reformation was fueled by disgust at the venality of the Roman Catholic Church in selling indulgences for the forgiveness of sins. In our own time much of that same venality is found in televangelists preaching a "prosperity gospel" that promises reward both now on earth and in the future in heaven.

A third inappropriate motive for giving is out of guilt. Once I was having dinner with a friend near Union Square in New York. Our table was right next to a window. While we were eating, a homeless couple with a small child settled in on the wide ledge right outside our window. While we ate, the little girl stood staring at us through the window. We both became very uncomfortable, and hurriedly finished our meal. On the way home each of us gave, somewhat begrudgingly, ten dollars to the family. I suspect if they had settled down for the night just one window over, we would have walked right by them without a second thought. We gave little, but just enough to assuage our guilt.

Godly Motives for Giving

There are, of course, other motives for giving. The first is simply to honor God. One of the unsung stories of the twentieth century is the rise of

---

1. Keefe, "Family That Built."

Christianity in China. When the Communists came to power in 1948, one of their first goals was to destroy religion. Temples, mosques, and churches were leveled. Religious leaders were imprisoned. Between 1948 and 1952, in one of the greatest martyrdoms in history, over two hundred thousand Christians were executed. At the time it was estimated that there were less than half a million active Christians left in the country, and many of those had been driven underground, forced to meet in secret. Yet when China was opened in the late 1970s, and the government allowed religious groups to again publicly worship, guess how many active Christians there were? Over fifteen million. Today that number is over one hundred million.

What explains this flowering? In 1952, there was a small community of Christians in Sichuan Province called the People of Jesus. They numbered less than thirty people. Times were hard. There were great food shortages and widespread famine. But the People of Jesus decided to give away half of what they produced. Why? Simply to honor God, to be good stewards. They had forty acres under cultivation, and by 1980 that forty acres was feeding three thousand people. It is among the most agriculturally productive plots of land in the world. Their own community had grown to over twelve hundred members. Their generosity was sufficient witness to God's love in Jesus Christ.

A second righteous motive for giving freely and unconditionally to help those in need. There is plenty of need, and the anguish of a single person should disturb those of us who say we love God. Because in God, we are all linked one to another. As John Donne wrote:

> No man is an island, entire of itself; every man is a piece of the continent, a part of the main. If a clod be washed away by the sea, Europe is the less, as well as if a promontory were, as well as if a manor of thy friend's or of thine own were: any man's death diminishes me, because I am involved in mankind, and therefore never send to know for whom the bell tolls; it tolls for thee.[2]

Jesus took this even further, in declaring his mystical connection with all who are suffering and in pain:

> Then the King will say to those on his right, "Come, you who are blessed by my Father; take your inheritance, the kingdom prepared for you since the creation of the world. For I was hungry and you gave me something to eat, I was thirsty and you gave me something to drink, I was a stranger and you invited me in, I needed clothes

---

2. Donne, *Complete Poetry*, 18.

and you clothed me, I was sick and you looked after me, I was in prison and you came to visit me." Then the righteous will answer him, "Lord, when did we see you hungry and feed you, or thirsty and give you something to drink? When did we see you a stranger and invite you in, or needing clothes and clothe you? When did we see you sick or in prison and go to visit you?" The King will reply, "I tell you the truth, whatever you did for one of the least of these brothers of mine, you did for me." (Matt 25:34–40)

It doesn't take much to heed this calling. One of my parishioners in Millbrook told me that growing up in Chicago he was involved with the Boy Scouts. He lived in a fairly poor neighborhood, and each year he went out with another man, collecting money to send scouts to camp. One day, they knocked at an apartment in one of the nearby tenements, and a young mother opened the door. She had a baby on each hip, her hair a mess, dress stained and wrinkled, the perfect image of domestic stress. My friend told her that they were collecting money to send scouts from the neighborhood to camp. She was silent for a few seconds, and then asked each of them to hold a baby. She then ransacked the apartment, and returned with a dollar and twenty-six cents. The two men eventually made their way back to scout headquarters, turned in all the money they had raised, and left for home. Forty minutes later they bumped into each other back at that woman's apartment door. Each was carrying two bags of groceries. Real generosity can be contagious.

A third godly reason to give is out of thanks. Thanksgiving begins with the understanding that everything we have is a gift from God. Once when I mentioned this to a very successful acquaintance, he responded, "That's just not true. I have worked hard for everything I have. I've earned my financial well-being. It's mine." This raised a few questions. Sure, it was true that he had worked hard, but where did his stamina and judgment come from? What about his courage and patience, let alone the support received from his family? Those things were given to him as God's gifts. As St. Paul said, when we're born we bring nothing into the world with us, and when we die we take nothing out (1 Tim 6:7). When we're alive, we have certain things. But they're not really our possessions. We are simply stewards of them. How we feel about those things and how we use them determines the quality of our life not only on earth, but perhaps for eternity.

My friend Harold Barrett told me a story that happened when he was rector of a church in Lookout Mountain, Tennessee. He was asked to meet with a couple he barely knew. When they sat down in his office, the husband said they were in the midst of a personal crisis and needed his guidance. Expecting the worst—an impending divorce, a wayward child, a serious illness—Harold said he would do what he could to help. The man said they had been deeply moved by how blessed they were. "We have a wonderful life," he said. "We're filled with joy with our family, and we have abundant wealth. We just want to do something to show our thanks to God. Will you help us to share our abundance with those in need?" Was that couple one in a million?

There are philanthropists who have given appropriately. His brutal response to the Homestead Strike in 1892 shows how ruthless Andrew Carnagie was in accumulating great wealth. Yet in retirement he became a model for responsible stewardship. He also wrote a widely read essay about generosity called *The Gospel of Wealth*. He plainly said the only purpose of being rich was to give money to enable people to help themselves. And he took that task with the utmost intentionality, writing, "It is more difficult to give money away intelligently than it is to earn it."[3] He thought anyone who died rich, died disgraced.

Giving Blesses the Giver

One of the most famous teachings of Jesus about wealth is that "It is more blessed to give than to receive" (Acts 20:35). Do you believe this?

A friend who was the pastor of a very large church in a Midwestern city once told me a story. He took pride in how carefully he managed his annual stewardship campaign with great care. The first year he was at this church, he met with several lay leaders to go through the list of those who had pledged the previous year. One name on the list surprised them. It was a lady in her late seventies who was physically disabled and on public assistance. She was raising three grandchildren, all under the age of ten, who were always clean, well fed, and neatly dressed. What surprised them was that she was one of the largest givers in the congregation. When they saw the amount she gave, they realized it was probably close to 25 percent of her income, far more than a tithe.

They decided to call on her and tell her that although they appreciated her generosity, because of her circumstances they were going to forgive her need to give at all. She sat in stunned silence before beginning to sob. "You have not only taken away my dignity," she told them, "you have taken away

3. Carnegie, *Autobiography*, 186.

my greatest joy." There is only blessing when we give freely, a joy that will never be known by those who are selfish and self-absorbed. This woman knew that. The men who had gone to see her were sensitive enough to realize their horrible blunder; they apologized and asked forgiveness. The fruit of her witness was that each of those men began to give sacrificially for the first time.

In the early 1970s Tom Bowers became rector of St. Luke's, a beautiful church in downtown Atlanta. Up until the 1920s, it was in one of the nicest residential neighborhoods in the city, surrounded by beautiful homes. But as decades passed, the residents moved away to nicer areas, often in the suburbs. Many of those homes were divided into apartments, and some were torn down and replaced by commercial buildings. Over a couple of generations, the neighborhood had completely transformed. The parish's immediate neighbors were drug addicts, prostitutes, and the homeless.

The church remained very strong and affluent, but the parishioners drove in from outside the neighborhood. Tom decided they needed to begin ministering to the people in their immediate environs, so began a feeding program for the homeless. They served lunch in their parish hall, a glorious room in an architecturally significant building. Within weeks, they were feeding several hundred people every week day. The room itself began to show the wear and tear, becoming a little shabby and rundown.

Some parishioners were extremely unhappy about this. One Sunday after church, a delegation of members approached Tom. Their leader, wagging a finger under Tom's nose, told him, "You are ruining our beautiful parish hall. I had my wedding reception in that room. My daughter had her wedding reception there as well. It's being destroyed. And I'll tell you something else: you aren't helping these people at all. I've been watching them. I see the same ones every week. They're not changing a bit. They're living the same lives they lived before, except now they have full bellies. I want you to stop this right now. This program is doing no good. It is not going to change a single one of those people." To which Tom replied, "Madam, the idea isn't to change them. The idea is to change you."

Just Do It

In his essay "Christian Behavior," from his book *Mere Christianity*, C. S. Lewis argues that if someone wants to be a Christian, the first step is simply to start acting as if one was a faithful Christian already.[4] When it comes to acting as a good, generous steward—someone who wants to grow into genuine faith—this may demand some risk. For almost all of us it will certainly demand a change in our behavior.

When I first moved to New York City in 1980, I had neighbors named Ted and Meredith Gandy. They were self-supporting missionaries in an inner-city ministry. They had to raise all their financial support themselves, and they lived close to the bone. One evening they told me that they had decided they were going to tithe their meager income. "It's already tough, and I don't know how we're going to accomplish this," said Meredith. "But we believe it is what God wants us to do, so we're going to do it. We'll just have to trust."

A year later we were together again and the topic of tithing came up. "It's been astonishing. Not in any spectacular way, but in small, quiet ways," Meredith told me. "Our kids were sick all the time before, and this year they've been completely healthy, so there have been no medical bills. Our car hasn't broken down. We decided to cancel our cable television. We chose to rarely eat out, even at McDonald's. Several of our supporting families gave us more than we expected. I'm almost embarrassed to say it, but we have more money now than we did last year before we tithed. We can actually have a family vacation this year."

I know another couple who recently went on a mission trip to Guatemala. They were a typical upper-middle-class family, living well but spending so freely they didn't feel like they had much extra income. In Guatemala, helping to build homes in an orphanage, they were completely captivated by the poor locals they met, who had such dignity and contentment with so little material wealth. During their week at the orphanage, the couple established deep, meaningful relationships with many of the children. Before returning home, they were asked if they would consider supporting ten children in one of the homes in the orphanage. The annual cost would be $25,000.

At first they laughed out loud. They had nowhere near that kind of discretionary money—they had a stiff mortgage and one child still in college. Besides, they were already giving generously to a variety of charities. But after they had been home for a few days, the wife asked her husband if he thought it might be possible for them to support the children. He chuckled, saying that he had been thinking about it almost constantly since they left

---

4. Lewis, *Mere Christianity*, 13.

Guatemala. They came to realize that the only way they could possibly do it was if they radically changed their lifestyle.

So they moved into a smaller house with a much smaller mortgage. They decided to limit eating out in restaurants and plan very simple vacations. By choosing to live more simply, they freed up enough income so they could easily commit to the support of ten children in the Guatemalan orphanage. When asked about their decision, they both said it was the most meaningful thing they had ever done. Nothing in their lives gave them more contentment and satisfaction. Perhaps Jesus was right. Perhaps it is more blessed to give than to receive.

Several years ago I saw an unforgettable television spot. The setting was the African bush. The camera panned across a gloriously beautiful wooded landscape to an open-sided tent. As the camera moved closer it revealed that this tent was a hospital ward. Bed after bed was filled with people who were suffering and dying. The camera stopped before one bed and zoomed in on a man writhing in pain, his body covered with open sores. It was shocking and chilling to see. Then the camera pulled back to another angle to show a young woman, a nun in full habit, sitting next to the bed, gently bathing the man's sores, comforting him in his agony. Suddenly a cynical voice-over cut in with someone saying, "I wouldn't do that for a million dollars." The nun looked up, directly into the camera, and said with a beatific smile, "Neither would I."

We are called to be generous. We are called to be good stewards. Stewardship is about freedom and joy. The imperative from God is simple. As you have freely received, freely give.

Chapter 9
Purity of Heart

Blessed are the pure in heart, for they will see God. (Matt 5:8)

Ron Underwood's 1991 film *City Slickers* tells the story of three friends who, dismayed by the approach of their fortieth birthdays, decide to go on a recreational cattle drive. It's a kind of boy's camp for men with nothing very exciting going on in their everyday lives. Leading the cattle drive is a rugged, wizened, fearsome old cowboy named Curly, played by Jack Palance. The whole adventure proves to be far more demanding and dangerous than the men had bargained for.

One night, as the men sit around a campfire, Curly falls into conversation with Mitch, an ad salesman, played by Billy Crystal. "Do you know what the secret of life is?" asks Curly, the light from the campfire twinkling in his eyes. "No, what?" responds Mitch. Holding up his index finger Curly went on, "This." "Your finger?' "One thing," Curly declares passionately. "Just one thing. You stick to that and everything else don't mean nothing." In exasperation Mitch asks, "That's great, but what's the one thing?" To which Curly replied, "That's what you've got to figure out."[1]

The One Thing

One of the most enduring legends in Western culture is the quest for the Holy Grail. Deep legend told of how the chalice from which Jesus drank

---

1. Underwood, *City Slickers*.

at the Last Supper was taken by Joseph of Arimathea to Britain. From the earliest centuries of the Christian era, stories were told in Christendom about the search for the chalice. It's a tale that has woven itself into popular culture over the course of centuries. Once, when I asked a group of children who was the only person to have found the Holy Grail, several boys shouted without hesitation, "Indiana Jones!" For most people the details of the real legend remain murky. I've asked that question on numerous occasions, and rarely has anyone known who in the tale actually found the grail.

There are many variations on the legend, but in the generally accepted narrative King Arthur has gathered together all the knights of the Round Table: Sir Lancelot, Sir Gawain, Sir Tristan, Sir Bedevere, Sir Percival and all the others. As usual, they are bickering about who is the greatest among them when suddenly, unexpectedly, they simultaneously see a vision of the Holy Grail. Each immediately sets off on a quest to find it, knowing whoever succeeded would be acclaimed the noblest of all knights. They have great adventures, suffer cruel hardships, and travel to far off mysterious lands. Yet in the end only one knight holds the Grail in his hands. He isn't the strongest, or the bravest, or the cleverest. As a matter of fact, he is only fifteen years old. It is Sir Galahad. He had only one characteristic that enabled him alone to find the Grail. He had purity of heart.

Purity of Heart

Purity of heart is a spiritual concept few understand. We all know what purity means in terms of material things: that they are clean, free from blemish, unadulterated. For years, Ivory soap presented its value with the advertising slogan, "99.9% pure." Pure what, exactly? The opposite of purity is to be dirty, filthy, and debased. No one would willingly buy a product that was impure.

The expression "purity of heart" calls to mind *moral* purity, being like someone who behaves impeccably under all circumstances. When we speak of a person as being pure, we would assume she was a person of honesty, goodness, generosity, holiness, and righteousness. In a religious sense such a person perfectly fulfills the will of God. Religious people have frequently equated purity with fidelity to a legal code, such as the Mosaic Law in Judaism (often referred to as the "Purity Codes"), the Sharia in Islam, or confessions of faith in Christianity. From there it can become a little more problematic, as "purity" may bleed into fierce, uncompromising moralism, or dogmatism intolerant of others.

That, however, is not at all what purity of heart means in the New Testament, or in Christian spirituality. Rather, it has a very specific meaning: *to be single-minded in devotion to God*. Purity of heart is to put nothing before devotion to God.

The New Testament covers this subject at length. Some of the teachings focus on what it is *not*. Purity of heart is not hypocrisy. A hypocrite is a person who says one thing, then does another. That is being double-minded, not single-minded. A dishonest person can't have purity of heart, for he or she is one who knows the truth but tells a lie, or one who knows what is right but does what is wrong. That too is being double-minded. Jesus wanted his followers to have purity of heart.

> As they were going along the road, someone said to him, "I will follow you wherever you go." And Jesus said to him, "Foxes have holes, and birds of the air have nests, but the Son of Man has nowhere to lay his head." To another he said, "Follow me." But he said, "Lord, first let me go and bury my father." And Jesus said to him, "Let the dead bury their own dead, but as for you, go and proclaim the kingdom of God." Another said, "I will follow you, Lord, but let me first say farewell to those at my home." And Jesus said to him, "No one who puts a hand to the plow and looks back is fit for the kingdom of God." (Luke 9:57–62)

That sounds pretty harsh, doesn't it? It's certainly not the kind of response I was taught in seminary while learning about pastoral care. But with purity of heart, one must be utterly single-minded.

Jesus' teaching consistently focused on single-mindedness. There's the story he told of three slaves who were each given money to invest by their master. Two of the slaves were single-minded in honoring their master's gift, investing wisely and giving back more than they had received. The third slave, however, was double-minded, worried more about loss than his responsibility, so he buried the money and returned the same amount he had received.

> "Then the one who had received the one talent also came forward, saying, 'Master, I knew that you were a harsh man, reaping where you did not sow and gathering where you did not scatter, so I was afraid, and I went and hid your talent in the ground. Here you have what is yours.' But his master replied, 'You wicked and lazy slave! You knew, did you, that I reap where I did not sow and gather

where I did not scatter? Then you ought to have invested my money with the bankers, and on my return I would have received what was my own with interest. So take the talent from him, and give it to the one with the ten talents. For to all those who have, more will be given, and they will have an abundance, but from those who have nothing, even what they have will be taken away. As for this worthless slave, throw him into the outer darkness, where there will be weeping and gnashing of teeth." (Matt 25:24–30)

Then there is the story of the rich young ruler who rushed up to Jesus and said, "Good teacher, what must I do to inherit eternal life?"

Jesus said to him, "Why do you call me good? No one is good but God alone. You know the commandments: 'You shall not murder. You shall not commit adultery. You shall not steal. You shall not bear false witness. You shall not defraud. Honor your father and mother.'" He said to him, "Teacher, I have kept all these since my youth." Jesus, looking at him, loved him and said, "You lack one thing; go, sell what you own, and give the money to the poor, and you will have treasure in heaven; then come, follow me." When he heard this, he was shocked and went away grieving, for he had many possessions. (Mark 10:18–22)

The young ruler went away with great sorrow. Why? Because he was double-minded. His money, his wealth, his possessions were more important to him than the kingdom of God. You cannot serve God and money. You cannot be double-minded and enter the kingdom of God.

Is It Worth the Cost?

Are you starting to feel a little uneasy? If entering the kingdom of God comes at such great cost, is it even worth it? Why would anyone want to be so single-minded? Why would anyone seek purity of heart? As Jesus said in the Beatitudes, "Blessed are the pure in heart, for they shall see God" (Matt 5:8). Seeing God? Finding the Grail? What is the value in that? Is it worth the cost? Well, the revelation that has come to us across history declares that those who have experienced the presence of God say two things. First, it is for that experience we were created. Seeing God is the ultimate experience of human existence. Secondly, no joy in all of creation compares to the joy of seeing God.

How valuable is it? Jesus himself told of a merchant who traded in jewelry all over the world. One day he found the perfect pearl, the "pearl of great price."

> "Again, the kingdom of heaven is like a merchant in search of fine pearls; on finding one pearl of great value, he went and sold all that he had and bought it." (Matt 18:45–46)

The merchant sold everything he had in order to possess that one perfect pearl. That is being single-minded. That is purity of heart.

But if you are still feeling a bit uneasy, you're in good company. Jesus' own disciples were uneasy. In reflecting on the rich young man, Jesus said,

> "Truly I tell you, it will be hard for a rich person to enter the kingdom of heaven. Again I tell you, it is easier for a camel to go through the eye of a needle than for someone who is rich to enter the kingdom of God." When the disciples heard this, they were greatly astounded and said, "Then who can be saved?" But Jesus looked at them and said, "For mortals it is impossible, but for God all things are possible." (Matt 19:23–26)

Impossible? Not for God. For God all things are possible. We can't save ourselves—we can't earn, or buy, or create purity of heart—but with God, all things are possible.

Time and again the greatest Christian saints and scholars have declared that seeing God, the "beatific vision," surpasses in value all other human experience. Dante wrote of this experience near the conclusion of *Paradise* in *The Divine Comedy*:

> Experiencing that Radiance, the Spirit
> Is so indrawn it is impossible
> Even to think of ever turning from It.
> For the good which is the will's ultimate object
> Is all subsumed in It; and, being removed,
> All is defective which in It is perfect.
> Now in my recollection of the rest
> I have less power to speak than any infant
> wetting its tongue yet at its mother's breast;
> and not because that Living Radiance bore
> more than one semblance, for It is unchanging
> and is forever as it was before;
> rather, as I grew worthier to see,
> the more I looked, the more unchanging semblance

appeared to change with every change in me.
Within the depthless deep and clear existence
Of that abyss of light three circles shown—
Three in color, one in circumference;
the second from the first, rainbow from rainbow;
the third, an exhalation of pure fire
equally breathed forth by the other two.
But oh how much my words miss my conception,
which is itself so far from what I saw
than to call it feeble would be rank deception!
O Light Eternal fixed in Itself alone,
by Itself alone understood, which from Itself
loves and glows, self-knowing and self-known.
that second aureole which shone forth in Thee,
conceived as a reflection of the first—
or which appeared so to my scrutiny
seemed in Itself of Its own coloration
to be painted with man's image. I fixed my eyes
on that alone in rapturous contemplation.
Like a geometer wholly dedicated
to squaring the circle, but who cannot find,
think as he may, the principle indicated—
so did I study the supernal face.
I yearned to know just how our image merges
Into that circle, and how it there finds place;
but mine were not the wings for such a flight.
yet, as I wished, the truth I wished for came
cleaving my mind in a great flash of light.
Here my powers rest from their high fantasy,
but already I could feel my being turned—
instinct and intellect balanced equally
as in a wheel whose motion nothing jars—
by the Love that moves the sun and other stars.[2]

The Way to Purity of Heart

In his book *Free of Charge: Giving and Forgiving in a Culture Stripped of Grace*, Miroslav Volf lays out the pathway of the Christian life in a remarkable way.[3] The book is in two halves, structured to reflect the life of God.

2. Dante, *Paradise*, 280.
3. Volf, *Free of Charge*, 19.

The first half, about giving, has three chapters: one on God the giver, one on Jesus as God's gift of salvation, and a third on the Holy Spirit as the one who empowers us to give. The second half of the book is about forgiveness. It too has three chapters. The first is about God the forgiver, the second is about Jesus as God's forgiveness, and the third is about the Holy Spirit as the one who enables us to forgive. Here's the rub: in the book Volf demonstrates step by step that—because of our sin, our self-absorption—it is impossible for us to give or forgive freely. For us everything is conditional.

That's why the most important chapter in each section is the third. Because it is only when we embrace what God offers us in Jesus Christ—it is only then when we are drawn into the very life of God—that the Holy Spirit begins to act through us. So when we give lavishly and freely, when we forgive those who have harmed us, it is actually God acting through us. The deepest human joy, the deepest experience of faith, is to realize that in the power of the Holy Spirit, God will live through us. The deepest human meaning, the most profound experience of faith, is to know that we can participate in God's redemptive love reaching into the fallen world. That is the pearl of great price. And that will only be fully known with the Holy Spirit's most astonishing gift, purity of heart.

The Heart of the Matter

It is in understanding what is truly at stake that the legend of the Holy Grail takes on such imaginative power. Who will find it? Not the one who is double-minded. Not the one who loves work, or family, or pleasure more than God. Can we first sell our field? No. Can we first bury our dead? No. Can we cling to our wealth as if it were our god? No. But if we are able to become single-minded about the kingdom of God, we may discover that we can trust Jesus. That if we seek first the kingdom of God, all these things will be added unto us. If, in God's grace, we can embrace purity of heart—not just when we are in great emotional need, but at times of clear sobriety—the doorway to God's kingdom will open before us. Think about your own life, about the decisions you make concerning how you spend your time, how you spend your money. Only the pure in heart will see God. Is that for you the pearl of great price? Would you give everything you have to make it your own?

Chapter 10

Praos

> *He entered a certain village, where a woman named Martha welcomed him into her home. She had a sister named Mary, who sat at the Lord's feet and listened to what he was saying. But Martha was distracted by her many tasks; so she came to him and asked, "Lord, do you not care that my sister has left me to do all the work by myself? Tell her then to help me." But the Lord answered her, "Martha, Martha, you are worried and distracted by many things; there is need of only one thing. Mary has chosen the better part, which will not be taken away from her."* (Luke 10:38–42)

WHEN I STARTED MY freshman year at the University of Wisconsin in Madison, I took a German language course with a dozen or so other students. About three or four weeks into the term, the entire class was given the assignment of translating a poem by Goethe into English. The poem was only eight lines and both the grammar and vocabulary were quite simple. When we came back to class the next day, each of us was instructed to write our translation on blackboards that covered three of the classroom's walls. I was astounded. Every translation was different. Not a single translation was the same.

That moment sparked my lifelong fascination with language, and the recognition that there are words and concepts in some languages that are impossible to translate with precision into others. I learned this intimately when I was pursuing my doctorate at the University of Edinburgh and had to pass examinations in five languages: French, German, Hebrew, Greek, and even Sanskrit. It was so difficult to find the right words to render any other language into English.

For Christians, accurate translations of the Bible are critically important because if, as we affirm, the Bible is the Word of God, then knowing exactly what it says is paramount. The work requires precision, care, and exactness with every translation from Hebrew, Aramaic, and Greek into English.

In the New Testament, this critical nuance is illustrated in the beginning of the Sermon on the Mount, called the Beatitudes. This is where Jesus says, "Blessed are the meek for they shall inherit the earth." As a passage, it's become so ubiquitous that we take it for granted, but as a message it flies in the face of everything we know about success, life, and happiness. We know the meek will not inherit the earth. So what exactly is Jesus getting at here? My trouble with the translation became even more apparent when one day I was reading the same passage in French. Where the English read "blessed are the *meek*," the French read "blessed are the *debonair*." If the same word in Greek means "meek" in English and "debonair" in French, then what was Jesus really trying to tell us?

The Greek word in question is πραεῖς, or *praos*, and its actual definition is so specific it demands erasing the word "meek" from your understanding. From now on you should only think, "Blessed are the *praos*, for they shall inherit the earth." What does *praos* mean? I spent a long time pursuing the meaning of this word, from the New Testament back into classical literature. As it happens, the word *praos* in classical Greek is used almost exclusively in relationship to horses. *Praos* means to break a wild horse. *Praos* means to train, to discipline, a powerful horse. *Praos* is a powerful, mighty horse under the control of its rider. It has very little to do with either meekness or being debonair. "Blessed are the *praos*, for they shall inherit the earth."

God Is the Rider

I have to admit, I know almost nothing about breaking a wild horse. What I do know about it I learned from watching cowboy movies as a boy. You know the scene where the tough cowboy dressed in buckskin from head to foot is determined to break a wild bronco? Boom, he hits the dust. He shakes himself off and gets on that horse again, and again, and again, and suddenly something miraculous happens. Suddenly the horse *is* broken.

Suddenly the horse is under the control of that rider and it will never again buck him off. He simply rides the horse out of the corral. "Blessed are the *praos*, for they shall inherit the earth."

Of course, breaking the horse is just the beginning. Once rideable, horses are also trained to respond to the commands of their riders. For ten years I lived in Millbrook, New York. When you hang around Millbrook long enough, you learn about riding, because it is an equestrian center in New York state. At least once each year, a famous Austrian riding instructor named Prince Karel von Auersperg came to run dressage clinics. We became friends and he often invited me to sit with him and observe his teaching. It was a lot of fun. Sitting behind a plate glass window overlooking the riding arena, he delivered his instructions over a microphone, always giving positive reinforcement. He would turn the microphone on and say something encouraging to the rider, and then shut the microphone off and turn to me and groan, "Terrible horse, worse rider."

Yet when both horse and rider were performing at an elite level, it was a thing of beauty to behold. What astounded me was that when Kari would give a command to the rider—to change from trot to canter, to suddenly go on a diagonal bias, to ride to a certain point and turn immediately to the right, and so on in flowing serpentine patterns—I would look intently at the rider and see no perceptible movement. Her hands wouldn't move. Her feet wouldn't move. She remained perfectly still. The horse would respond immediately to what must have been the slightest command. A movement, a shift in weight so slight I wasn't even able to observe it with my own eyes. A horse that is so disciplined and trained is a horse that has *praos*. "Blessed are the *praos*, for they shall inherit the earth."

But what did Jesus mean when he said it? Just this: we are the horse and God is our rider. The wild, undisciplined, headstrong horse must be broken, and the same is true for us. When God breaks us, it's called "repentance": we give control of our lives over to God, and God disciplines us. Under the hand of the Holy Spirit, we are trained to respond to the call of God. The Christian life, the life of sanctification, is learning how to discern the almost imperceptible cues so that we will know God's will and be able to respond to it. We are the horses. God is the rider. God wants to ride us into the world, the world God created, to establish God's kingdom, to bear witness to God's justice, righteousness, peace, and love. "Blessed are the *praos*, for they shall inherit the earth."

We Are the Rider

One of my favorite books is *The Great Divorce* by C. S. Lewis, a wonderful, spun-out metaphor contrasting hell and heaven, told in very modern terms and language. Hell is a dark, dank, dreary, drab industrial city, populated by miserable, shadowy beings. There is bus service between hell and heaven, running continuously and free of charge. Anyone in hell can step on a bus and be taken right to the verge of heaven. But most don't want to get on this bus. The very few who do are extremely uncomfortable as they get closer and closer to heaven because they are drawn out of their shadowy drabness to take on a luminosity and density that terrifies them. Even so, some make the journey.

Near the end of *The Great Divorce*, one of these specters who has made the journey gets off the bus and starts walking very slowly toward heaven.[1] A red lizard is perched on his shoulder. The lizard is jabbering little things in his ear. The man is approached by a great angel, powerful and bright, who tells him, "You cannot bring the lizard into heaven." The man doesn't like that idea. "This lizard has been with me my entire life," he responds. "This lizard tells me what to do. I can't survive without this lizard. I have to bring him with me." The angel says, "You may not bring the lizard into heaven. If you like, I will kill him for you." Suddenly the lizard's eyes pop wide open. "He's lying. If he kills me, it will kill you," it screams. "Don't let him kill me!" The man, confused and conflicted, is caught in a powerful desire to enter heaven. He tries to pull the lizard off. The screaming red monster digs his claws into the man's flesh. The angel speaks to him again saying, "I will kill him for you."

In despair, the screeching lizard digs his claws deeper into the man's shoulder. Finally, the man nods yes to the angel, and with one great blow the lizard and the man are struck unconscious on the ground. Maybe the lizard was right; maybe they are both dead. Then, slowly, the man begins to stir. He is transformed from his pale shade, taking on light, luminosity, density. As he rises up on his feet, he looks just like the angel. Then the lizard begins to stir. It begins to grow in size, density, and luminosity as it transforms into a huge, great stallion, which the man mounts and rides into heaven.

In Lewis's metaphor the lizard represents our passions—the passions that control us, our obsessions, our compulsions, the things we are afraid to give up to God. Jesus doesn't call us to anything but a death that leads to

---

1. Lewis, *Great Divorce*, 100.

a new life, a life beyond a life we know now. "Blessed are the *praos*, for they will inherit the earth."

Seeking *Praos*

When I was at Grace Church in New York City, I once hosted a dinner party for a number of young parishioners to meet the Pulitzer Prize–winning historian Robert K. Massie. Although these young people were working at various kinds of jobs, each had the self-identity of being a writer and each was eager to learn from him. Massie had one question for them: "How much time do you spend writing every day?" A young woman responded by saying she was experiencing writer's block and hadn't been able to write anything for over six weeks. He responded, "Then don't call yourself a writer. It doesn't matter if you are published or not. A writer writes. If you don't write, you are not a writer."

Something similar could be said about Christian faith. What does it mean to be a Christian? A Christian is one who loves God and neighbor. If our faith has any validity, we will act on it. When we don't act on it in pursuing spiritual disciplines or in service to others, we are in the grip of sloth, whether we want to admit that or not. What would the world be like if there was no sloth? What would American society be like? What would your life be like? There is a virtue, neither well known nor understood, that points to that one thing, to an entirely different way to live.

As humans, we have a number of practices and disciplines that can lead us to a sense of happiness, contentment, and confidence, and relieve us of the torpor of sloth. Rigorous physical exercise not only tones and tightens muscles; it releases endorphins in the brain that replace lethargy and ill ease with well-being. Being disciplined in meditation or practicing a craft with expertise can bring peace and order to one's inner life. Conscientiously managing our time, prioritizing tasks, and acting on them in a disciplined way creates an energy and assurance that will bolster self-esteem and win the respect of others. Any person, with or without religious faith, can adopt and practice such natural virtues and enjoy their benefits.

Praos, however, is not a natural virtue. It can only be achieved through faith and grace, because there is no other access to intimacy with God. We become fully human—we fulfill our destiny—when our full being, our intellect and will, our emotions and imagination, our consciousness and psyche, are given over to God. In such a state we can respond to even God's slightest urgings. Just like a great horse ridden by a dressage master, we are called by God to *praos*. We are called by God to become people who are not undisciplined and wild, but broken and disciplined by God, our King.

Learning to Listen to God

This is all easier said than done. How are we to embrace *praos* in relationship to God? Even though it is not a natural virtue, and ultimately it can only be known in grace, there are spiritual disciplines that prepare us to receive it.

One aspect of this should be obvious: anyone who wants to be directed by the voice of God must learn to be silent. How else will you hear what God may be saying? I have spent much of my parish ministry doing spiritual direction, the technical term for teaching people how to pray. The vast majority of people, even those with an active piety, have to be taught how to become silent before God. That is because most prayer is a discursive monologue—us telling God what *we* need or want for ourselves or others. The principle at the heart of this prayer is that we are doing the talking, and very often we never even pause to hear if God may be saying something back to us.

There is no question that discursive prayer—as intercession and petition, or even as praise and thanksgiving—is valid. But none of those modes of prayer will lead to *praos*, let alone hearing God or discerning God's will. There is a great lesson on this that comes to us from 1 Kings in the Hebrew Bible. Fleeing the wrath of King Ahab and Queen Jezebel, hiding in a cave, the prophet Elijah passionately sought to hear the voice of God.

> He said, "Go out and stand on the mountain before the Lord, for the Lord is about to pass by." Now there was a great wind, so strong that it was splitting mountains and breaking rocks in pieces before the Lord, but the Lord was not in the wind; and after the wind an earthquake, but the Lord was not in the earthquake; and after the earthquake a fire, but the Lord was not in the fire; and after the fire a sound of sheer silence. When Elijah heard it, he wrapped his face in his mantle and went out and stood at the entrance of the cave. Then there came a voice to him that said, "What are you doing here, Elijah?" (1 Kgs 19:11–13)

God was not in the whirlwind. God was not in the earthquake. God was not in the fire. God was in the sheer silence. We must learn the discipline of being silent before God, of maintaining silence before God, if we are ever to hear God's voice, if we are ever to enter into *praos*.

Chapter 11

Patience

> *May you be made strong with all the strength that comes from his glorious power, and may you be prepared to endure everything with patience and good courage, while joyfully giving thanks to the Father, who has enabled you to share in the inheritance of the saints in the light.* (Col 1:11–12)

ONE OF THE THINGS that I love most about baseball is that, though it is a team sport, each game turns on a one-on-one, personal confrontation between the pitcher and the batter. Who wins those little contests within the game depends on a number of factors, but the three most crucial are talent, preparation, and patience. I once witnessed a classic confrontation between John Franco of the Mets and Barry Bonds of the Giants, the most fearsome hitter of his generation. Here's the situation: It's the ninth inning, the score is tied, there are two outs, and the bases are loaded. John Franco throws a series of nasty pitches, almost all of which are strikes. Yet, all the while, Barry Bonds stands at the plate calmly and confidently. He intentionally fouls off pitch after pitch while he patiently waits for that one pitch that he can drive deep into the outfield. When that pitch arrives, he's ready, and he drives it to the right field wall, scoring the winning run. Why did it happen? Patience.

The Power of Patience

If you ask someone to name a virtue, it's likely to be patience. After all, the expression "patience is a virtue" is used so often it's shopworn. Yet of all the Christian virtues, I think this may be the one most misunderstood, because so many people feel that patience is a sign of weakness or passivity. In reality nothing could be further from the truth. Patience is epitomized by the calm, cool, confidence of Barry Bonds at the plate. The patient individual is never reactive, never overwhelmed. Patience allows one to remain in control, actively and intelligently waiting for the appropriate moment to act. As with the other virtues we have been discussing, there are no barriers to patience; it is certainly not something that is exclusively reserved for people of religious faith. Patience can be manifested by people from any background, under all circumstances.

One of my favorite movies is David Lean's 1957 Academy Award–winning *The Bridge on the River Kwai*. The setting is a Japanese prisoner of war camp in Burma, where the inmates are forced to build a railroad bridge, for use by the Japanese military. The commandant of the camp, played by Sessue Hayakawa, is a brutal, sadistic monster with absolutely no concern for the value of human life. The British prisoners, in his opinion, are worse than slaves, and he will do anything to squeeze the maximum amount of work out of them, at the least cost to himself. Many of them are beaten and worked to death.

But a British POW named Colonel Nicholson, played by Alec Guinness, arrives at the camp and absolutely refuses to give in, no matter how irrational or murderously violent the Japanese commandant becomes. Colonel Nicholson patiently, ever so patiently, insists that the Japanese must honor the Geneva Accords. He will not concede. He never wavers. Time after time—calmly, firmly—he insists that the Japanese treat the British soldiers with dignity and provide them with adequate shelter, food, and medical care. In the course of the movie, there is an amazing shift of power. By the end of the film, for all intents and purposes, the British colonel is running the POW camp, a sign of the strength of patience.

A more contemporary example is the story of South Africa's Nelson Mandela. Arrested in 1963, this man spent nearly thirty years in prison. Why? Because he insisted that all human beings should have equal rights, regardless of race. He was simply defending a right that Americans take for granted, that's built into our Constitution. His dream was to build a non-racist society in South Africa through the democratic process, and for thirty years he never wavered from this dream.

When he was finally released over thirty years ago, in 1990, Mandela was under unbelievable pressure to seek revenge—many of his countrymen insisted that the White South Africans must be subjected to the same kind of pain they had inflicted on Blacks and colored, and be destroyed in a bloodbath of violence. But Mandela—clearly and calmly, with the same kind of patience he showed in prison—kept to his vision, never wavering in his commitment that justice and equality must be guaranteed for every human being, regardless of race. His victory in the elections in South Africa in 1994 was not only a magnificent triumph for the human spirit; it is a classic example of how patience, far from being weak, is in reality the ground of true strength.

Biblical Patience

In the Hebrew Bible, the patient were seen to be the most righteous of God's chosen. The patient could endure any hardship because they trusted in the ultimate goodness of God. The prime example is Job, who is described as being a man of patience no less than thirteen times in that short book. Though he suffered unbelievably agonizing pain and tragedy, Job never wavered in his trust in God.

In the New Testament, the Greek word that is translated as patience is *upomone*. It can also be translated as "endurance," "perseverance," or "steadfastness." My favorite rendering of it is "good courage." *Upomone* in a Christian is powerful and liberating, but for ordinary people confronting the ordinary circumstances of everyday life, it may be the most helpful virtue of all.

Patience and Frustration

In my own experience, patience is especially necessary when we are in the grip of frustration. For two years when I was in seminary, I worked as a night watchman on a vacant college campus in exchange for an apartment. We lived in a complex of dormitories where other seminarians, also watchmen, had apartments for their families, arrayed around a courtyard. Our closest friends were a couple named Rock and Suzanne Doddridge, who had a little boy about four years old, named Jonathan. One evening, as I was studying near an open window, I could hear Rock calling his son to come in for dinner. I heard his call several times, and I would look up to see Jonathan still playing in the courtyard, ignoring his father. I also noticed Rock's calls becoming a little angrier each time Jonathan didn't move. Finally, there was a loud bang as Rock burst out of the door, picking up his son and yelling, "I told you to come in ten times!" He carried Jonathan back toward their apartment, disappearing through the door.

When I looked out about a minute later, Jonathan was back out in the courtyard with a look of determination on his face. I knew that Rock had a volatile temper, so I sat back to wait and see what would happen. But it wasn't Rock who came out of their apartment. It was Suzanne. She walked over to Jonathan, sat down, and they talked for a minute before she actually began to play with him. I couldn't hear what she was saying, but I could tell she was not confronting or challenging him in any way. After a couple more minutes, mother and son got up together and walked hand in hand back into their home.

The whole situation intrigued me, particularly about how Rock had responded. The next day I asked him about it. He was a little embarrassed, but he admitted that when he discovered Jonathan had defied him and had gone out of their apartment a second time, he was ready to detonate. Suzanne intervened, saying, "Rock, let me talk to Jonathan, but please do something for me first. I want to lay your hands on me and pray that God will give me patience." Rock told me that through that prayer, his anger shifted into an entirely different mode of being, in which he experienced a quality of patience that let him give authority over Jonathan to Suzanne. That prayer, in turn, enabled Suzanne to actually accomplish what they wanted, in love, not anger.

Patience and Revenge

Patience is also the virtue we need when we have that desire to strike back, the desire for revenge, the compulsion to settle the score. I've thought about this, and I think this is particularly true in our relationships with our families, with business associates, or in committees on which we serve. In moments of conflict, we are usually sufficiently well socialized that we don't respond to a disagreement by getting up and smacking someone in the face. We are far subtler than that: we simply go for the put-down, insist on having the last word, or seethe with passive aggression. Do you know what I'm talking about?

When I'm in this particular kind of conflict, I am almost always caught up in a cycle of demanding to have the last word. I've actually watched myself do this, when I insist something should be done one way, and someone else counters that it should be done another way. Even when it is obvious that we have arrived at an impasse—or maybe even after a decision has been made—I still have to explain why I'm right, one last time. Often, someone will pick up the bait, and he'll insist why he is right. And the cycle begins again: because I can't let him have the last word, I have to explain yet again why I'm right. Soon we are further apart than ever, locked into simmering, seething anger.

Several years ago I was on an extremely contentious diocesan committee. People disagreed about almost everything. There was one woman on the committee who had a very strong personality. But in time I noticed that she would always simply state her case, present why she thought something should be done, and even though others continued to argue, she was perfectly content to leave it at that. Fairly recently, we were at a meeting in which the other committee members were aggressively challenging her. At least three times over the course of the meeting she was given an opportunity to put somebody down or have the last word, but she said nothing. She just looked at them and smiled. I was so intrigued, I asked her about this afterward. It was really very simple. She felt that if she had adequately stated her case once, it didn't need to be said again. She had the confidence that among fellow Christians, if her views were presented with clarity, God's will ultimately would be done.

Patience and Depression

Patience is also the virtue we most need when we get into a mindset where life feels unendurable, where everything inside us becomes barren and desiccated, or we feel we just have to escape into something new. As a young man I had a very dramatic conversion to Christian faith, and for about fourteen months my life was so exciting spiritually I felt the constant presence of God. I spent joyful hours every day studying and praying and learning about the nature of God and about faith. My life was more exhilarating than it had ever been before.

Then suddenly, after a little more than a year, it was as if the presence of God was withdrawn. When I would read the Bible, my mind would drift. When I would pray, it was as if I was in an empty barren place. It frightened me. My initial reaction was that maybe my faith had been some kind of psychological projection. Maybe there was no God. I went to see a friend, a man named Bob Salinger, who was far more mature in faith than me. I explained to him what was happening, that my entire structure of faith had collapsed. Instead of being empathetic the way I had expected, he laughed. "Well, Ken," he told me, "maybe now you will let God build something real, something eternal inside of you."

At the time, I didn't understand what he meant, but I did keep praying and studying and stayed in Christian fellowship. I discovered that after a season God did return to me in new ways. I have now been involved in a life of faith for over fifty years, and there have been many times of hollowness when I felt I had no sense of the presence of God. But I have learned if I remain patient, and if I remain disciplined and faithful to a life of prayer, to a commitment to worship through liturgy, to study and to ministry, in time God will come in fresh and surprising ways.

As a matter of fact, I have been through this cycle so often now that when I enter a period of aridity, my patience is fueled by the knowledge that I am actually learning *more* about God when God is absent than when God is present. There are four things that can be learned only when God is absent. The first is discernment of what is spiritually valid and what is invalid. The second is the true nature of grace. The third is the true nature of God, which can only be known in silence. And finally, how humility is the primary virtue leading to intimacy with God. I know now that it is a blessing to give myself over to patience, because patience leads to endurance, and endurance leads to strength, and strength gives us the ability to maintain fidelity under difficult circumstances.

Patience and Fear

Patience is also the virtue we need when we are so overwhelmed by fear, all we want to do is either strike back or flee, fight or flight. No one personified this more forcefully than Martin Luther King Jr. Andrew Young, the civil rights leader and politician, tells a story about a flight he and King took together from Atlanta to Birmingham. After the plane was in the air, Dr. King had a panic attack. He started to sweat and pant. He got up from his seat to pace up and down the aisle. Young, who was a young man in his twenties at the time, didn't know what was going on.

When he finally calmed down, King told him that he had these panic attacks all the time because he knew that someday he would meet a violent death. He had three choices: he could give up his ministry, and stop presenting himself in a society that was hostile, by running away; he could give into those who were more radical than he, and resort to violence as the path to equality; or he could remain patient. In spite of his personal terror, because of his faith King was able to be patient. He endured, facing fears that were both inner and outer. He maintained, through consistent patience, fidelity to the dream of racial equality in America through nonviolence.[1]

Seeking Patience

Do you ever get frustrated? Do you ever find yourself in a situation where you want to strike back, even if it is just verbally? Do you ever find yourself feeling so bereft you wonder if it's worth going on? Are you ever so overwhelmed with fear that you just want to run away? If any of those things sound familiar, the primary Christian virtue you should seek is patience. But how do we get it?

It's just like the other virtues: it is a gift of grace that can't be bought, learned, or in any way achieved. But it can be received. It is a gift that God wants to give us, and we must seek it in prayer. Spiritual memory is like muscle memory. If we make asking God for patience a centerpiece of our life of prayer, our consciousness will be slowly transformed. We will find praying for patience will be on our lips when we truly need it, in any circumstance, day by day, week by week, year in and year out. In the New Testament, Paul links patience to faith and hope no less than four times. It is not in any way passive or weak. It is actually the virtue that will give us the greatest confidence and strength to meet whatever the world throws at us.

---

1. Menand, "When Martin Luther King."

Chapter 12

Wisdom

> *For wisdom is better than jewels,*
> *and all that you desire cannot be compared with her.* (Prov 8:11)

IF YOU FOUND YOURSELF in serious trouble, and you wanted to go to someone for help and advice, to whom would you go? If you can actually think of someone, I have a second question: What is it about that person that would lead you to entrust yourself to him or her?

In my experience, two criteria stand out as the most important. First, I would go to a person who desires only what is best for me. Secondly, I would seek a person who has the wisdom to help me find an appropriate solution. Do you know anyone like that, anyone with such wisdom? Wisdom, I'm afraid, is a virtue that is a rare commodity in our world.

Natural Wisdom

The very word "wisdom" is of interesting derivation. According to the *Oxford English Dictionary*, the concept of wisdom was first used as a suffix, such as in the words "likewise" and "crosswise." The root meaning is "a habitual manner of life, leading to the capacity to make right judgments concerning life and conduct."

Like all the other virtues, wisdom is not restricted to a certain type of person. The wise among us come in all shapes and sizes, and wisdom is in no way limited to those with religious faith. Even those with no spiritual perspective at all can still display great wisdom.

This natural wisdom has two aspects. The first is an intuitive sense of the good, the beautiful, and the true. This is the wisdom displayed by outstanding artists and athletes. The second aspect of wisdom I call "discretion": the ability to sort through a myriad of options to find the right way to move forward. That wisdom is most highly prized in business and the professions. When we look at how wisdom manifests itself naturally, I am struck by how narrowly it is focused. If we view wisdom as *only* the intuitive grasp of the good, beautiful, and true, we can search all history and find no more than a handful of people who manifested wisdom in all three of those areas. As a matter of fact, people who display wisdom in just one area are bound to be successful. If they have wisdom in two, we would probably grant them the title of "great."

Several years ago, I watched a documentary that featured Pablo Picasso, toward the end of his life, when he was in his late eighties. As he was taking a camera crew through his studio, they came to the last painting Picasso had completed. It was magnificent. "How long did it take you to create this?" asked the interviewer. The old man looked right into the camera and said, "I took me my whole life."[1] Everyone would agree that Picasso showed wisdom of genius when it came to understanding the true and beautiful. But if you know anything about his personal life, he did not manifest much wisdom about the good.

Which brings us to the other aspect of natural wisdom, discretion, the ability to cut through masses of information to find proper solutions. If you were ill, you would certainly hope that your doctor had discretion as he or she was trying to arrive at a diagnosis. There is no question that Elon Musk is a person of tremendous wisdom when it comes to making visionary business decisions leading to massive amounts of money. But few would argue that he has any wisdom when it comes to the good, the true, or the beautiful.

Several years ago I read a biography of Learned Hand, the great federal judge whom some consider to be the outstanding American jurist in history. The book describes Judge Hand as a man whose understanding and interpretation of constitutional law was the very epitome of wisdom. His airtight briefs and judgments were written with such beauty and clarity that the legal community still holds him in awe. Yet when it came to his personal life, Judge Hand was filled with confusion and disappointment.[2]

1. Clouzot, *Mystery of Picasso*.
2. Gunther, *Learned Hand*, 59.

Many people in the professions, business, and the arts display genuine wisdom. But more often than not, this wisdom is narrowly focused. Where are the people who display wisdom in every aspect of their lives? Do you know any? If you do, I'd like to meet them.

Christian Wisdom

When it comes to Christian wisdom, we move into an entirely different realm. Like the other Christian virtues, wisdom has two aspects that make it unique. First, it opens us to the presence of God. Second, if we receive the wisdom of God, we know immediately that it is a gift of grace. You can't buy it; you can't learn it; you can't achieve it.

Biblically, no virtue was more highly prized than wisdom. Solomon was given the option of choosing whatever gift he wanted from God. In choosing wisdom, he became the model, the rule, the paradigm of a godly leader. There is an entire category of books in the Hebrew Bible called Wisdom Literature. It comprises the Psalms, Proverbs, Ecclesiastes, Job, Song of Songs, and Ruth, all books that are focused on how to live a godly life. Later on in Israel's history, wisdom came to be personified as the feminine presence of the divine among us, *chokma* in Hebrew and *sophia* in Greek. Wisdom was also considered to be one of the primary attributes of Jesus. St. Paul wrote,

> For Jews demand signs and Greeks desire wisdom, but we proclaim Christ crucified, a stumbling-block to Jews and foolishness to Gentiles, but to those who are called, both Jews and Greeks, Christ is the power of God and the wisdom of God. For God's foolishness is wiser than human wisdom, and God's weakness is stronger than human strength. (1 Cor 1:23–25)

Christian wisdom does share the first two aspects of natural wisdom. We Anglicans are richly blessed, because to my mind nothing more perfectly expresses the good, the beautiful, and the true—the reality of God and our salvation—than the *Book of Common Prayer*. Most of the time, we simply read or listen to these liturgies without much mindfulness. But every word in this book is so carefully weighed, every turn of phrase is so considered, that the reality of faith is captured in full. And every one of its liturgies reflects wisdom. Every liturgy presents the truth and beauty of God's plan of salvation, and the goodness of God's redemptive love.

Discretion, the second aspect of wisdom, manifests itself in the Christian life particularly as it applies to stewardship. We are called to live a godly life. We are called to live a manner of life in which we give of our time, talent, and money. As twenty-first-century American Christians, we may display the greatest lack of wisdom in this when it comes to time management. Are you ever subject to the tyranny of time? Do you ever say to yourself, "I just don't have enough time"? You know what? Time is the great equalizer. It might come as a surprise to you, but everybody has the same amount of time. There are only twenty-four hours in each day. Bill Gates isn't rich enough to buy a twenty-fifth hour. Vladimir Putin doesn't have enough power to wrest a sixty-first minute out of reality. Do you know what the difference is between highly effective people who get things done on time and done well, and people who are run ragged and can never seem to finish any project? It is simply the ability to manage time with discretion.

Increasingly, I have come to see time management as a spiritual discipline. When people come to me for formal spiritual direction, I will tell them that if we enter this relationship, they have to give me an hour a day for prayer. How would you respond? How many of you would laugh in my face, or say, "Are you kidding?!? I don't have enough time as it is." Well, I know that if a person is willing to offer every twenty-four-hour period to God, and is willing to bring intention to making priorities, anyone can find an extra hour a day.

I know something else. When I think back about my life, one of the most stressful periods was when I was first married. At the time, I was working over forty hours a week in a hospital, taking two courses to finish my undergraduate degree, had a house and lawn to care for, and working in a prison ministry three nights a week. Every Sunday when I looked at how the next week was going to unfold, I would be filled with anxiety. How could I ever do it all? But I learned that as I offered that time to God, there was always enough to do what had to be done. There was never any time to waste, but there was always enough time. A wise person, a person of godly wisdom, will find the time.

Discernment

There is another aspect of wisdom that is utterly unique to those of religious faith. This is discernment, the ability to discern the will of God, the ability to know, regardless of circumstances, God's will. In Christian piety, few things are as confusing as discernment. Several misconceptions need to be laid to rest if we are to have a true perception of it.

To begin with, I have met people who will not act until they can discern God's will with clarity and exactness. This is a mistake. In reality, God's will often emerges only as we take risks and act—we will have no certainty beforehand, but only discover certainty as we move forward. When I was a young priest, working at St. Bartholomew's in New York City, I was offered a job to run a research center for the World Council of Churches, monitoring new religious movements. I had recently completed my doctoral dissertation on Hinduism in the West, and was establishing a reputation as an expert on new religious movements. It seemed like the ideal position for me. I would direct a staff of a dozen researchers who published a journal every month. I would be sent by the Council all over the world to brief Christian leaders on what was happening in new religious movements. It also came with an appointment as a university lecturer.

There was one major obstacle: this research center was in Aarhus, Denmark. So I actually sought and used the discipline of discretion. I visited Aarhus, met the people there and liked them. I consulted with my wife, who told me she was open to moving. As I tried to come to a solution, I listed all the pluses and minuses. I prayed and weighed and finally decided to take the job. I called the people in Aarhus and Geneva to tell them I'd accepted their offer. I told my boss, Tom Bowers, I would be leaving St. Bartholomew's. I went home that night with peace in my heart. My older brother, David, stopped by the house and we talked it over. As we were talking, I realized I had made a terrible mistake. I didn't want my children to grow up in a foreign country. I could clearly discern God was calling me to a career in parish ministry. I just didn't know it until after I had made the commitment to go.

Another myth about discerning God's will is self-reliance, the belief we can discern God's will all on our own. When I first came to a genuine Christian faith, I joined a charismatic Jesus People fellowship in Wisconsin called the Madison Prayer and Praise Community. Many members emerged as leaders there, the most intriguing of whom was a man named Peter Olsen. He looked like a completely strung-out hippie, but he was the most courageous Christian I have ever met. He would go right into the lion's mouth and bear witness to Jesus. He won some notoriety in Madison when he stood up in a meeting of Students for a Democratic Society and spoke out about the love of God in Jesus.

One night Peter came to the community and said that the Holy Spirit had revealed to him that he was to quit his job as a baker's helper and work full-time as an evangelist. The community was to pay him a salary. Peter was a very convincing guy with a powerfully charismatic personality. I was so impressed that I started to dig into my pocket to pull out my wallet. Then another of the leaders, Bob Salinger, a resident psychiatrist, walked over to Peter, looked him squarely in the eye, and said, "The Holy Spirit hasn't said that to me." We can only have certainty in discerning God's will if it is confirmed by others in the body of Christ.

Another myth concerning discernment is the idea that there is only one answer. Years ago, my friend Bob Massie had a dual teaching appointment at Harvard Business School and Harvard Divinity School. An ordained Episcopal priest, Bob began to feel that God was calling him to enter public life by running for office in Massachusetts. His primary concern was to know God's will, and so we entered into intense spiritual direction for six weeks to try to discover an answer. Should he stay in his teaching position where he had just been given tenure, where he knew his family would have security, or should he run for public office? One or the other. Finally, early in November, he called and said God had given him the answer. The answer was remarkable. "It doesn't matter what you do," God said to him. "I will be with you." Very often if we discern God's will, we see that a whole variety of responses may be appropriate.

Another misconception is that once God's will is known, no one will have the power to resist it. I discovered the very opposite is true. When I perceive God's will, those are the most incredibly liberating moments of my life. God sets us free to make responsible decisions, and it is almost a rule for me that if I feel coerced, or if I feel I'm being manipulated, or that I have no other option, it is almost certainly not God's will. God comes to set us free. When we know God's will, we are able to make responsible choices as adult men and women of faith. We will be able to move forward, perhaps not with certainty, but knowing that God will be with us.

Yet there are other times when discerning God's will comes as revelation with startling clarity. Years ago I had a conversation with someone who had been on a search committee for a new rector at his church in Virginia. It was a large church with many talented, successful people in the congregation. Beginning with a pool of over a hundred candidates, the search committee cut it down to twenty, and then whittled it down some more until, after fourteen months of work, they had four finalists. At what they thought was to be their last meeting, they intended to choose their new rector. Once the meeting opened, it became immediately obvious that none of the candidates was appropriate. Some were passionate about this candidate, but others said they would leave the church if that one was called. The committee was completely hamstrung.

The chairman of the committee went home heartsick. It was late and he went into his study, pulled out the long file drawer with all 130 candidates' resumes. He felt like tossing them in the garbage. But underneath them, at the bottom of the file drawer, he found another candidate's profile, one that had been misplaced fourteen months before. He had never opened it, but as he read this person's theological statement, description of his piety, and his vision for ministry, there was tingling all up and down his spine. He was absolutely certain that this was the person God wanted to lead them into the future.

At the time this candidate was still in his early thirties. The next night the chairman called a meeting of the search committee and presented this profile. They invited him to come visit, and after the interview a miracle happened: everyone on the committee said yes. They gave thanks and praised God that they had failed the week before, because it prevented them from making a mistake. Sometimes God's will is revealed to us with a clarity beyond reason, and we discern it in extraordinary ways.

A Wisdom Different from That of the World

There is a story, now with many iterations, that has circulated among particular groups of Christians for several generations. It took place on an ocean liner crossing the Atlantic around the turn of the century. About a week out, the evening entertainment was to be a talent show. Some passengers sang, others played instruments, and a few danced. But the highlight and culmination of the evening was to be a contest in public speaking. The winner of this event would receive a crown of laurel leaves.

Although two or three competitors had already given their speeches, everyone in the audience was waiting with eager anticipation for the final speaker, a famous English actor. He was tall, handsome, elegant, and held the room in rapt attention as soon as he stepped to the stage. He then recited the Twenty-Third Psalm with such eloquent beauty that when he finished, the passengers responded with spontaneous acclamation. He was proclaimed the winner and given the crown of laurel leaves.

In the din that followed, few people noticed that an old, poorly dressed man took the stage after the actor had left. No one knew anything about him. In fact he was a retired Christian missionary traveling home, third class, after forty years of service at a mission station in West Africa. He began to speak, and slowly the crowd quieted. He spoke so softly that some people had to strain to hear him. Soon they realized that he too was reciting the Twenty-Third Psalm. As he said those familiar words very simply, very plainly, without any flair—"The Lord is my shepherd, I shall not want . . . He maketh me lie down in green pastures . . . Yea, though I walk through the valley of the shadow of death, I will fear no evil . . . Thy rod and thy staff shall comfort me . . ."—a kind of preternatural silence took hold of the whole room.

The silence continued after the old man had finished speaking, only broken by the English actor, who returned to the stage, took off the laurel crown, and placed it on the old man's head. "I know the psalm," he said, "but you know the Shepherd." Each witness in that room was changed by the experience. Years later, many who were there said that in those simple, plain words of that godly man they heard the voice of God.

That is a story we need to hear too, in the twenty-first century. Why? Because in many ways our church is in danger of allowing the simple power of the gospel to be suffocated by worldly wisdom, an eloquent, intellectual understanding that comes from two sources.

Despite the ubiquitous insights of pop psychology and business strategies, Christian salvation is not about self-realization, self-actualization, or possibility thinking. It is not about figuring out how to establish ourselves emotionally and materially on the path of unending success. But if you were at home right now, surfing through YouTube, you would be hearing that message time and again from Christian speakers. That is not what the gospel is about. The gospel, Christian salvation, is not about material success; it is about living faithfully in relationship with God.

There is also a danger, not so much individually but collectively, of the church allowing the power of the gospel to be choked by business considerations. If a church wants to grow, to become vital, the last thing it needs is a public relations consultant, or a marketing strategy. Yet this is exactly what many churches do. If we as a church are to become what God wants us to be, we must have a clear and simple vision consisting of three parts: we are to be a place where people come to faith, we are to be a place where people experience a forgiving and compassionate community, and we are to be a place where God's love motivates us to go out into the world to serve those in need. Faith, community, and witness. That is what pleases God. That is what God desires for the church. We don't need public relations or marketing for that.

And so this leads us to a final source of worldly wisdom threatening the gospel, both in our time and throughout history. It is the church itself. It is the church that pushes the special interest of some to the center, so that we divide into quarreling camps. That divisiveness is a denial of the simple gospel of unity in Jesus Christ.

Several years ago I attended a reception at the Century Club in New York City. It was a black-tie affair, but I chose to wear a clerical collar. It is always interesting what strangers will tell you at events like that if they know you are a priest. One man approached me whom I'd never met before, although I recognized him because he is well known as a public figure. Without batting an eye, he proceeded to tell me why he was not a Christian, listing a whole series of the sins of the church. As I listened to him, I had to say with honesty that he was right, and that there are times when I say the Creed and come to the place where we are called to say, "I believe in the holy catholic church . . ." and it makes me want to gag.

My teacher Bob Munger once said that Jesus Christ suffered three humiliations. The first was the incarnation. The second was the crucifixion. And the third is the church. According to Karl Barth, perhaps the twentieth century's greatest theologian, said the last great obstacle to the kingdom of God on earth is the church.[3] Do you believe that? Well, Dr. Barth wasn't done. He also maintained that the church is also the place where the redemptive love of God is most visibly manifest.

Both those things are true. We are called to be a church where simple faith, compassionate community, and loving witness are our only measures of success. If we can learn to live the simple gospel, like the retired missionary on that ocean liner, our witness will reach out beyond us to the world. Many will be able to say, "There, at that place, we can hear the voice of God." But that will happen only if we as the church learn to discern the wisdom of God.

---

3. Barth, *Faith*, 139.

Chapter 13
The Way Home

> *As God's chosen ones, holy and beloved, clothe yourselves with compassion, kindness, humility, meekness, and patience. Bear with one another and, if anyone has a complaint against another, forgive each other; just as the Lord has forgiven you, so you also must forgive.* (Col 3:12–13)

THERE IS A BASIC double premise behind this book. The first principle is that all of us are caught up in patterns of sin and self-absorption. This self-absorption leads to unhappiness and, according to the Bible, alienates us from God, from others, and even from our own true selves. The state of sin is not just pervasive; it is the fundamental human condition, and this inevitable self-absorption manifests itself in a whole variety of attitudes and behaviors.[1] The consequences of sin are not just chaos and discontent in our present lives. On the contrary, since we are accountable to God for everything we do, the consequences of our sinful behavior is enduring. It doesn't have to be this way. The second principle in this double premise is that God created us to embrace virtue. A virtuous existence will not just make us happy; it will open us to intimacy with God and others. That too will have eternal consequences. As St. Paul wrote to the Galatians,

> Do not be deceived; God is not mocked, for you reap whatever you sow. If you sow to your own flesh, you will reap corruption from

---

1. For a full treatment of no less than ten categories of sin, see my book *Into the Wilderness: Understanding the True Nature of Sin.*

the flesh; but if you sow to the Spirit, you will reap eternal life from the Spirit. (Gal 6:7–8)

If, however, we accept this premise, how can we move from sin and alienation to grace and virtue? How can we move from pride to humility, or from despair to hope? If the human condition is self-absorption rooted in sin, how can we possibly undo this self-destruction and become open to unconditional love? The Christian answer is plain and simple. There is nothing we can do. Fortunately, God has done it for us. But before addressing that, we must first understand the nature of sin.

The Human Dilemma

We have all known what it feels like to be happy, content, and at peace in ways that open us to well-being and joy. But all of us are also touched by evil, whether through physical pain, mental anguish, or moral wickedness. And the consequence of all that evil is suffering. This can take different shapes. There is natural evil, which is the result of certain contortions in creation, ranging from disasters like volcanoes and hurricanes to illnesses such as cancer and schizophrenia. And there is moral evil, which is the result of human choice. Evil exists, and even agnostics and atheists who refuse to acknowledge God must cope with the indignity and suffering it causes.

The reality of evil forces us to ask questions of meaning. How do we explain it? What is the cause of evil? Nature asserts that it is simply a consequence of evolution and the competition for survival. Psychological explanations focus on personality disorders, past trauma, and the manipulative dynamics of personal relationships. Sociological descriptions look to social origins such as poverty, discrimination, and the lack of education and healthcare. All these approaches explain what evil is, but they all fail to answer why it exists in the first place.

The Bible provides another explanation. As Cornelius Plantinga has written:

> Every person suffers. Our pain ranges from annoyance, loneliness, boredom, anxiety and futility to rage, alienation, paralysis, terror and despair. The Christian affirmation is that our misery is caused by sin. It is sin that distorts our character, corrupting our human faculties of thought, emotion, will and imagination. Sin

both causes and results from our misery of aloneness, restlessness, estrangement, shame and meaninglessness.[2]

According to Scripture, sin is the ultimate cause of evil, the source of our unhappiness and suffering. And we remain both accountable to God for it and impotent to overcome it.

But we are not without hope. After all, the story of the Bible declares God loves us and has not abandoned us. While we may want God to be a benevolent, sentimental Santa in the sky, giving us whatever we desire, such a wish is not only self-absorbed; it would not be a relationship based on love. Confronted with human sin, God's love is like a crucible, refining the ore of our being, separating the good from the bad. God must find a way for us to freely abandon our sin. In the end, this opens the possibility of something far greater than we could have ever imagined, because, "unlike other identifications of human trouble, a diagnosis of sin and guilt allows hope. Something can be done for this malady. Something has been done for it."[3]

God's Plan of Redemption

That something is the plan of salvation God inaugurated in the fall. There were immediate, painful consequences when Adam and Eve turned their worship from God to self. The intimacy that had been the source of their joy and love was shattered and replaced with alienation, anguish, and shame. No longer able to be vulnerable or intimate, Adam and Eve tried to cover their nakedness with leaves and hide from God and one another by slinking from tree to tree. They refused to take responsibility for their own actions. Adam blamed Eve, declaring to God, "The woman you gave me made me do it" (Gen 3:12). Eve blamed the serpent. Strife, struggle, and suffering constituted the new reality of their existence. Cut off from the eternal, irrepressible life of God, their new existence could only end in death. And they had no ability, no power to undo the consequences of their choice. They could do nothing to restore the lost life-giving intimacy with God.

In the midst of that bleak, despairing turmoil, God inaugurated the first step of a plan to redeem fallen humanity and restore us to divine intimacy. Genesis 3:21 states,

---

2. Plantinga, *Not the Way*, 5.
3. Plantinga, *Not the Way*, 5.

> And the Lord God made garments of skins for the man and for his wife, and clothed them.

That simple, seemingly obscure verse is so significant some theologians have referred to it as "the hinge of history" because it declares that God has *not* abandoned sinful humanity. In the grip of shame, crippled by their nakedness and vulnerability, Adam and Eve could no longer bear to go on living. So God intervened, covering their nakedness with the skins of animals and relieving their shame. The cost was high, as life itself had to be sacrificed; blood had to be shed. It was a sacramental act whose meaning pointed to the future, a future where another life would be given up, and more blood shed in order to redeem the sins of all humanity.

But that was just the inauguration of God's plan. Later came the promise to redeem humanity from sin, which was consecrated through the covenant God made with Abraham.

> "I will indeed bless you, and I will make your offspring as numerous as the stars of heaven and as the sand that is on the seashore. And your offspring shall possess the gate of their enemies, and by your offspring shall all the nations of the earth gain blessing for themselves, because you have obeyed my voice." (Gen 22:17–18)

Over five hundred years later, during the exodus, God renewed the promise with Abraham's descendants who had become the nation of Israel.

> "Now therefore, if you obey my voice and keep my covenant, you shall be my treasured possession out of all the peoples. Indeed, the whole earth is mine, but you shall be for me a priestly kingdom and a holy nation. These are the words that you shall speak to the Israelites." So Moses came, summoned the elders of the people, and set before them all these words that the Lord had commanded him. The people all answered as one: "Everything that the Lord has spoken we will do." Moses reported the words of the people to the Lord." (Exod 19:5–8)

Still, the people of Israel continually failed to keep the covenant, chasing after other gods and often flaunting the Law that was to be the sign of their fidelity.

But God remained faithful; over time the promise changed as three streams of redemptive prophecy emerged in Israel's later history. The bearer of redemption would no longer be the entire nation, but a single descendant of King David, to be known as the *Messiah*: "I will establish the throne of his kingdom for ever" (2 Sam 7:13). Another prophetic stream saw the promise of redemption fulfilled in a direct divine intervention at the end of history by one called "the Son of Man" (Dan 7:13-14). The third prophetic tradition proclaimed that the fulfillment of God's promise would come through one known as the "Suffering Servant," who would bring redemption by suffering on behalf of the people (Isa 53:4-6).

Furthermore, the prophet Jeremiah proclaimed that God's promise of redemption would demand a divine intervention to not only destroy sin but give humanity a new identity,

> The days are surely coming, says the Lord, when I will make a new covenant with the house of Israel and the house of Judah. It will not be like the covenant that I made with their ancestors when I took them by the hand to bring them out of the land of Egypt—a covenant that they broke, though I was their husband, says the Lord. But this is the covenant that I will make with the house of Israel after those days, says the Lord: I will put my law within them, and I will write it on their hearts; and I will be their God, and they shall be my people. No longer shall they teach one another, or say to each other, 'Know the Lord', for they shall all know me, from the least of them to the greatest, says the Lord; for I will forgive their iniquity, and remember their sin no more. (Jer 31:31-34)

Of course, the gospel message is that all these promises of God, carried across history by Israel, were fulfilled in Jesus Christ. Christians declare that he was the Messiah—not the military hero expected by Israel, but the Messiah who was also the Son of Man and the Suffering Servant. In one marvelous passage from Mark's Gospel, all three redemptive strands were braided together in a single exchange between Jesus and his disciples,

> Jesus went on with his disciples to the villages of Caesarea Philippi; and on the way he asked his disciples, "Who do people say that I am?" And they answered him, "John the Baptist; and others, Elijah; and still others, one of the prophets." He asked them, "But who do you say that I am?" Peter answered him, "You are the *Messiah*." And he sternly ordered them not to tell anyone about him. Then he began to teach them that the *Son of Man* must undergo great *suffering*, be rejected by the elders, the chief priests, and the scribes, and be killed, and after three days rise again. (Mark 8:27-31, emphasis added)

Jesus was Emmanuel, God become human, but free from sin. As John the Baptist realized, he was the pure lamb who was to die in the place of sinful humanity: "Behold the Lamb of God who takes away the sins of the world" (John 1:29). Sin was atoned for, but the act of redemption was the sacrifice of God's own self for us through Jesus Christ.

Jesus' resurrection opened the meaning of God's redemption. He was the second Adam, perfectly fulfilling the will of his Father in heaven. It was his shed blood on the cross, his absolute, unmitigated sacrifice, that broke the power of sin over mankind. If the core of sin was self-absorption, Jesus' act of unconditional love cosmically shattered the grip sin had on humanity. It is what C. S. Lewis called the "good infection," spreading through the power of the Holy Spirit to all who put their faith in Jesus.[4] With sin's hold over us broken, the power of death was destroyed, and God's promise to redeem humanity was fulfilled. After ascending into heaven, Jesus sent the Holy Spirit to bring new life to those who believed in him. And he promised to come again, to finally consummate the promise of redemption with the resurrection of all humanity for judgment followed by the recreation of heaven and earth.

For humanity—suffering from the consequences of evil and impotent to undo the damage—the gospel is truly "good news." But its power turns on understanding and believing that sin is the source of our unhappiness. As Cornelius Plantinga has written,

> Unless we acknowledge the reality of sin, the gospel makes no sense: The music of creation and the still greater music of grace whistle right through our skulls, causing no catch of breath and leaving no residue. Moral beauty begins to bore us. The idea that the human race needs a Savior sounds quaint.[5]

How Do We Enter Redemption?

Whenever I'm asked why I am a Christian, I always respond that it's because I know I need a savior. For anyone who acknowledges his or her own sinfulness, the gospel message is nothing short of amazing grace. For this new life—this new creation made manifest in Jesus' resurrection—is offered as a free gift of grace to every human being. It is a universal salvation, open to everyone. The key question in every religion, however, is how to move from the universal to the particular. Anyone stirred by the biblical vision

---

4. Lewis, *Mere Christianity*, 149.
5. Plantinga, *Not the Way*, xii.

will immediately ask, "How can I make the great redemptive narrative of the Bible *my* story?," "What must I do to make God's plan of redemption personal, for me, make it mine?," or at its most basic, "What must I do to be saved?" The answer is simple to understand and difficult to do. Jesus opened his ministry by declaring,

> "The time is fulfilled, and the kingdom of God has come near; *repent*, and *believe* in the good news." (Mark 1:15)

Or as on the day of Pentecost, when the crowd asked what they must do to be saved, Peter replied,

> "*Repent*, and *be baptized* every one of you in the name of Jesus Christ so that your sins may be forgiven; and you will receive the gift of the Holy Spirit. For the promise is for you, for your children, and for all who are far away, everyone whom the Lord our God calls to him." (Acts 8:38–39, emphasis added)

It sounds simple, doesn't it? Believe, repent, and be baptized. But that begs further questions. The first is: What does it mean to believe? For starters, to enter God's salvation, we must believe the gospel. But that's not all. As Reinhold Neibuhr has written,

> Human beings desire security, but we feel restless and anxious because we are both finite and free, limited and unlimited. Yet our base problem is unbelief. Failing to trust in an infinite God, we live anxiously restless, always trying to secure and extend ourselves with finite goods that can't take the weight we put on them. Unbelief leads to anxiety leads to dominating pride and sensuality.[6]

The second question is: What does it mean to repent? Repentance is an act of the will, a basic movement from self toward God. The Greek word for repentance, the word used in the New Testament, is *metanoia*. Literally it means "to turn around 180 degrees." Quite simply, repentance is turning from self to God. It begins with an acknowledgment of our own sinfulness, and of our own accountability to God. Sincere repentance requires penitence and contrition. Penitence is mourning for the sin one has done, coupled with the resolve to sin no more. Contrition, in the words of Bernard of Clairvaux, is "heavy and grievous, sharp and poignant in the heart." Because repentance demands both complete honesty and utter transparency, it may be the most acutely personal thing any of us can do.

---

6. Neibuhr, *Nature*, 83–86.

The final piece of the puzzle of salvation, following belief and repentance, is baptism. It is possible, and certainly not uncommon, for individuals to enter a relationship and even deep intimacy with God on their own, but both Scripture and Christian tradition testify that spiritual health is to be found primarily through the fellowship of the church. Jesus commissioned the apostles to be his agents in proclaiming the gospel and validating God's forgiveness for the repentant,

> Jesus said to them again, "Peace be with you. As the Father has sent me, so I send you." When he had said this, he breathed on them and said to them, "Receive the Holy Spirit. If you forgive the sins of any, they are forgiven them; if you retain the sins of any, they are retained." (John 20:21–23)

The apostles also inaugurated the sacramental ministry of the church, which centered the redemptive reality of Jesus within the faith community. Baptism became the vehicle for binding a believer into the redemptive forgiveness of God. This is why the baptismal liturgy begins with a formal repentance called the three renunciations:

> Do you renounce Satan and all the spiritual forces that rebel against God? Do you renounce the evil powers of this world which corrupt and destroy the creatures of God? Do you renounce all sinful desires that draw you from the love of God?[7]

This is followed by three affirmations of belief:

> Do you turn to Jesus Christ and accept him as your savior?
> Do you put your whole trust in his grace and love?
> Do you promise to follow and obey him as your Lord?[8]

Thus is fulfilled Jesus' initial imperative, "Repent and believe in the good news" (Mark 1:15). In non-liturgical traditions, baptism is usually preceded by a similar formula in what is often popularly called the "Sinner's Prayer," entailing confession, repentance, and an affirmation of Christian faith.

Baptism, of course, is not the end but the beginning of Christian life. Although we enter a new relationship with God through belief, repentance, and baptism, we will inevitably again fall into sin. In acknowledging this, the challenge in the baptismal liturgy is very clear: "Will you persevere

---

7. *BCP*, 299–308.
8. *BCP*, 451.

in resisting evil, and, whenever you fall into sin, repent and return to the Lord?" It is not "if" you fall into sin, but "whenever" you fall into sin. The promise of the believer is: "I will with God's help."

In the Catholic tradition there is also a formal liturgy of confession, usually in a private session between an individual and a priest. It provides an opportunity for those who are grievously troubled by their sin to share their concerns, and receive spiritual counsel. The priest may suggest concrete acts of penance before formally offering absolution. In *The Book of Common Prayer* this liturgy is called "The Reconciliation of a Penitent." It ends with these words said by the priest"

> There is now rejoicing in heaven; for you were lost, and are found; you were dead, and are now alive in Christ Jesus our Lord. Go in peace. The Lord has put away all your sins. (p. 451)

But while there is joy in heaven over the true repentance of each sinner, my experience is that very few Christians who repent experience that joy personally. There are exceptions, of course, but for the majority, living out the rhythm of a life of faith is far more an objective duty than an affective, life-giving experience. There are three reasons for this. The first is that many Christians only superficially wrestle with their own sinfulness in confession. They may go through the motions, either privately or liturgically, never fully engaged intellectually, emotionally, or spiritually. Secondly, most Christians have also never learned to be still and silent before God, so they have never been in position to experience the forgiveness God is offering. The third reason most Christians do not experience forgiveness in a powerful way is because seeking God's forgiveness is just the first step in a three-part process. Most Christians think about forgiveness only in terms of being forgiven by God. But the full Circle of Forgiveness will only be known when two more steps have been taken.

The Full Circle of Forgiveness

After a believer has accepted forgiveness from God through personal repentance and baptism, there are two further steps in the circle of redemption. The next is to forgive those who have harmed us—something every Christian knows, if rarely practices with any deliberate intention. This is in spite of the fact we declare it out loud every time we publicly worship, from the Lord's Prayer:

> Father... forgive us our sins, as we forgive those who have sinned against us.

The final step, which may be the most difficult of all, is to seek forgiveness from those whom we have harmed. It is only when we embrace all three of these steps—forgiveness from God, forgiving others, and seeking forgiveness from those we have harmed—that the circle will close and the full power of God's freedom and joy may be known. When all three are woven into a seamless pattern of personal piety and spiritual discipline, the circle will be unbroken.

Forgiveness from God

Forgiveness is an objective reality, and takes place whether or not one feels any sense of joy. Yet it must be reiterated that unless a person truly repents with intentionality, penitence, and contrition there will be little or no feeling around it. As Claudius mused in Shakespeare's *Hamlet*,

> My words fly up, my thoughts remain below:
> Words without thoughts never to heaven go . . .
> Bow, stubborn knees, and heart, with strings of steel,
> Be soft as sinews of the new-born babe![9]

I reiterate, the reality of forgiveness is objective—a believer must look beyond his or her own psychological and emotional state, and believe that God's forgiveness comes through repentance. As Paul wrote to the Romans,

> We do not live to ourselves, and we do not die to ourselves. If we live, we live to the Lord, and if we die, we die to the Lord; so then, whether we live or whether we die, we are the Lord's. For to this end Christ died and lived again, so that he might be Lord of both the dead and the living. Why do you pass judgment on your brother or sister? Or you, why do you despise your brother or sister? For we will all stand before the judgment seat of God. For it is written, 'As I live, says the Lord, every knee shall bow to me, and every tongue shall give praise to God.' So then, each of us will be accountable to God. (14:6–12)

As the Bible teaches and the creeds affirm, we await a Judgment Day when every human being will be resurrected and stand before God. That is the witness of all three Abrahamanic religions, Christianity, Judaism, and

---

9. Shakespeare, *Hamlet*, act 3, scene 1.

Islam. But the biblical testimony concerning judgment is so heavily laden with eschatological symbolism that we attempt to truly understand it at our own peril. But if we strip away the symbolic language, certain themes emerge. As John wrote in the book of Revelation,

> And I saw the dead, great and small, standing before the throne, and books were opened. Also another book was opened, the book of life. And the dead were judged according to their works, as recorded in the books. And the sea gave up the dead that were in it, Death and Hades gave up the dead that were in them, and all were judged according to what they had done. Then Death and Hades were thrown into the lake of fire. This is the second death, the lake of fire; and anyone whose name was not found written in the book of life was thrown into the lake of fire. (Rev 20:12–15)

Christian faith asserts that Jesus is both the Judge and the Redeemer, and that through his crucifixion, he took the sins of all humanity into himself. In him sin was destroyed, death itself was annihilated, replaced by eternal life. That is the plain gospel: our sins are washed away in the blood of the Lamb.

Try to envision being at Judgment Day, and everyone is standing before the judgment seat of God in groups of three. If you had a choice, would you rather be standing between Adolf Hitler and Attila the Hun, or between Mother Teresa of Calcutta and Francis of Assisi? Well, it won't make a bit of difference, because ultimately everyone is saved by grace.

True repentance requires a willingness to face the consequences of our sinful behavior. One of my early Christian mentors was Edward West, longtime canon liturgist of the Cathedral of St. John the Divine in New York City. He once told me about an incident from years earlier, during his tenure as rector of Trinity Church in Ossining, New York. One night, he was awakened from a deep sleep by pounding on his front door. He opened the door to discover a highly agitated young man demanding to see a priest and confess his sins. Canon West invited him in and agreed to hear his confession. He began by reciting the liturgy "The Reconciliation of a Penitent to the man:

> The Lord be in your heart and upon your lips that you may truly and humbly confess your sins: In the Name of the Father, and of the Son, and of the Holy Spirit. Amen.

The man nearly shouted out, "Father, I have just murdered a man. Please, please, give me absolution." In recounting this story, Canon West asked me, "Ken, what would you have done in that situation?" I hemmed and hawed before admitting I didn't know. He countered that there was only one correct response: "I told the man, 'Come with me right now to the police station, and turn yourself in. Then I will give you absolution.'"

It should go without saying that repentance requires utmost honesty—even if the church has been duped, God will not be. Paul Thomas Anderson's 2007 movie *There Will Be Blood* features one of the most chilling scenes of modern cinema, in which Daniel Plainview (played by Daniel Day-Lewis) publicly and cynically repents in order to win a lease for his oil pipeline. "I am a sinner," he cries out. "I have abandoned my child. I have abandoned my child. I have abandoned my boy."[10] By the end of the film, he is rich beyond measure, but at the cost of total alienation. Wallowing in mindless drunkenness, he gets his revenge by beating to death the minister who baptized him. With his false repentance he rejected forgiveness and absolution, and suffered the consequences.

It is not enough just to repent for what we have done, however, because we are also accountable for what we have left undone. How often do we look past the needs of others, smugly comfortable within our own self-indulgence? This is in spite of the fact Jesus himself left us with a fierce, uncompromising admonition"

> "When the Son of Man comes in his glory, and all the angels with him, then he will sit on the throne of his glory. All the nations will be gathered before him, and he will separate people one from another as a shepherd separates the sheep from the goats, and he will put the sheep at his right hand and the goats at the left . . . Then he will say to those at his left hand, 'You that are accursed, depart from me into the eternal fire prepared for the devil and his angels; for I was hungry and you gave me no food, I was thirsty and you gave me nothing to drink, I was a stranger and you did not welcome me, naked and you did not give me clothing, sick and in prison and you did not visit me.' Then they also will answer, 'Lord, when was it that we saw you hungry or thirsty or a stranger or naked or sick or in prison, and did not take care of you?' Then he will answer them, 'Truly I tell you, just as you did not do it to one of the least of these, you did not do it to me.' And these will go away into eternal punishment, but the righteous into eternal life."
> (Matt 25:31–45)

God will not be mocked.

---

10. Anderson, dir., *There Will Be Blood* (2007).

Forgiving Others

As difficult as it is to acknowledge and truly repent of our own sins, forgiving those who have harmed us is an even more galling prospect. Even when the insult or injury is slight, it can be an excruciatingly onerous and distressing task, for a variety of psychological and spiritual reasons. We simply don't want to make ourselves vulnerable again to someone who has already harmed us—our natural impulse is to strike back, whether out of a sense of justice, or revenge, or self-protection. Perhaps in no other area is the Christian moral imperative more contrary to human nature. But there is no escaping the imperative:

> "Love your enemies and pray for those who persecute you . . ." (Matt 5:44, 6:14–15)

> "For if you forgive others their sins, your heavenly Father will forgive you; but if you do not forgive others, neither will your Father forgive your sins . . ." (Mark 11:25)

> "Whenever you stand praying, forgive, if you have anything against anyone; so your Father in heaven may forgive you your sins. Be merciful, just as your Father is merciful. Do not judge, and you will not be judged; do not condemn, and you will not be condemned. Forgive, and you will be forgiven." (Luke 6:36–37)

To forgive is not to condone bad behavior, or to deny that harm has been done. As Jesus reminded his followers, we are called to stand against evil and rebuke sin, while still prepared to forgive the sinner.

> "Be on your guard! If another disciple sins, you must rebuke the offender, and if there is repentance, you must forgive. And if the same person sins against you seven times a day, and turns back to you seven times and says, 'I repent,' you must forgive." (Luke 17:3–4)

There are some Christians who have not understood this. "I can forgive, but I cannot forget, is only another way of saying I will not forgive," wrote Henry Ward Beecher. "Forgiveness ought to be like a canceled note—torn in two, and burned up, so that it never can be shown against one."[11]

But that misunderstands the nature of redemption. Joni Mitchell was wrong—redemption is not innocence, and God does not want us to go back to the garden. Redemption means looking forward and always

---

11. Beecher, *Big Book*, 108.

remembering the cost. The iconic symbol for this is Jesus bearing the wounds of the crucifixion on his risen body. As Paul Tillich has written,

> Forgiving presupposes remembering. And it creates a forgetting not in the natural way we forget yesterday's weather, but in the way of the great "in spite of" that says: I forget although I remember. Without this kind of forgetting no human relationship can endure healthily. I don't refer to a solemn act of asking for and offering forgiveness. Such rituals as sometimes occur between parents and children, or friends, or man and wife, are often acts of moral arrogance on the one part and enforced humiliation on the other. But I speak of the lasting willingness to accept him who has hurt us.[12]

In truth, the refusal to forgive—the suppression of powerful emotions like resentment, anger, and festering malice—may have grave psychological repercussions, eating away any sense of contentment and joy. When we nurture animosity against someone, it binds us to them in ways that cripple and enslave us. Miroslav Volf has written about being a young man in the Yugoslavian army, when he was brutally interrogated by someone he refers to as "Captain G." The abusive questioning made him reel with fear and feel "that as a person, I was nothing."[13] Once he was set free, Captain G continued to torment his memory:

> It was as though Captain G. had moved into the very household of my mind, ensconced himself right in the middle of its living room, and I had to live with him. I *wanted* him to get out of my mind on the spot and without a trace. But there was no way to keep him away, no way to forget him. He stayed in that living room and interrogated me again and again.[14]

Volf discovered he would be set psychologically free by learning to forgive. But that freedom is simply a prelude to love—the ability to love those who have hurt us. This is at the center of the great mystery of forgiveness. It unlocks our hearts so we can love. And as Paul reminded the Corinthians, it was for love we were created:

> As God's chosen ones, holy and beloved, clothe yourselves with compassion, kindness, humility, meekness, and patience. Bear with one another and, if anyone has a complaint against another,

---

12. Tillich, *Eternal Now*, 32.
13. Volf, *End of Memory*, 6.
14. Volf, *End of Memory*, 7.

forgive each other; just as the Lord has forgiven you, so you also must forgive. (Col 3:12–13)

Forgiveness can take place as an inner transaction, intentionally, before God, letting the malice go from the deep inner sanctums of heart and mind. But it can also demand personal interaction. On several occasions in my life, I have felt the holy imperative to forgive someone face to face. Some of those times did not result in a positive emotional reconciliation, but rather a brittle acknowledgment that forgiveness had taken place. For me, the blessing was being set free from the resentment I had harbored. That freedom, as a gift of grace, is priceless. But even if there is no release in the act, take comfort in the words often attributed to Oscar Wilde:

Always forgive your enemies—nothing annoys them so much.

Seeking Forgiveness from Others

The third and final piece of the mystery of forgiveness is acceptance of the fact that we have harmed others, and that we must seek their forgiveness in order for us to enter the full radical freedom to which God calls us. Sometimes there will simply be no way to achieve this; some people we will have lost contact with years ago; others may even have died. In these cases all we can do is offer our shame and contrition to God, and ask God to bless the particular person.

When I was in college, I did something cruel that still haunts me. During rush at my fraternity, I was taking a potential pledge through the house, and I decided he wasn't up to our standards. So I led him out on the second-floor fire escape and shut the door behind him. There was no way to get back in the building, so he would have had to climb down a ladder to the ground. My act was completely cruel, and it must have left the young man quaking with humiliation and rage. I never even learned his name, and I'm certain I'll never see him again. But when that memory creeps into my consciousness, I offer my shame to God and ask that he bless that man. He must be in his mid-seventies now.

Sometimes getting in touch with a person we've harmed will only add insult to injury, so discretion and discernment must be exercised. But if we can connect, the godly imperative is that we should. The healing power of forgiveness forms the core of the twelve-step programs, such as Alcoholics

Anonymous. In particular, steps 8 and 9 focus on seeking out those whom we have harmed:

> 8. Make a list of all persons we have harmed, and become willing to make amends to them all.
>
> 9. Make direct amends to such people wherever possible, except when to do so would injure them or others.[15]

There is a risk involved in doing this, as there always is when we make ourselves vulnerable to those who may hate us, and may welcome an opportunity to do us harm. Anyone who embarks on this discipline must anticipate getting clobbered. After all, look what happened to Jesus. All we can do is tell the truth, humbly seek forgiveness, and give the relationship over to God.

One of the great political and social triumphs of the twentieth century was the creation of the Truth and Reconciliation Commission by the newly elected democratic government of Nelson Mandela in South Africa in 1995. Under the leadership of Archbishop Desmond Tutu, the Commission brought together the perpetrators and victims of violence under apartheid, with the goal of healing, not just for individuals but for the whole nation. As Tutu declares, those who seek forgiveness bless the victim as well as themselves,

> . . . the process of forgiveness also requires acknowledgement on the part of the perpetrator that they have committed an offense . . . Take the Cradock Four, for example. The police ambushed their car, killed them in the most gruesome manner and set their car alight. When, at a TRC hearing, the teenage daughter of one of the victims was asked: would you be able to forgive the people who did this to you and your family? She answered, "We would like to forgive, but would just like to know who to forgive."[16]

Howard Thurman, perhaps America's greatest theologian in the twentieth century, declares the significance of forgiveness and reconciliation in this prayer:

> Whatever disaffection there is between me and those who are or have been very close to me—I would seek the root or cause of such disaffection, and with the illumination of Your mind, O God, to understand it. I give myself to Your scrutiny that, whatever there

---

15. W., *Big Book*, 59.
16. Tutu, Vanderbilt address, 2003.

may be in me that is responsible for what has happened, I will acknowledge. Where I have wronged or given offense deliberately or without intention, I seek a face-to-face forgiveness. What I can undo I am willing to try; what I cannot undo, with that I seek to make my peace. How to do these things, what techniques to use, with what spirit—for these I need and seek Your wisdom and strength, O God. Whatever disaffection there is between me and those who are or have been very close to me, I lay bare before You.[17]

This is a clarion call, for if Christians won't embrace ministries of reconciliation, who in our society will? When we find ourselves in the midst of conflict, we are called to love, to be peacemakers, to seek forgiveness and reconciliation. That is far from easy. It demands humility and vulnerability. But that's the key, because as we empty ourselves in this way, in the mystery of faith we become united to Jesus in his passion. Jesus himself will be with us.

These three steps constitute the true vision of Christian reconciliation: being forgiven by God, forgiving those who have harmed us, and seeking the forgiveness of those whom we have harmed. But for a Christian, this is not an end in itself. It simply opens the door to a new life, a life of growing in faith, a life of witness to the truth of the gospel in both in what we say and what we do. That life turns on understanding and embracing the virtues that will enable us to become what God created us to be.

The Pursuit of Virtue

When the Circle of Forgiveness has been completed, the real work begins. With the pursuit of virtue, we can enhance our intimacy with God, and equip ourselves for ministry in the world. But virtue can be known fully only in contrast to sin. Just as sin is what separates us from God and alienates us from others, virtue is what nurtures the new redemptive life offered to us through the death and resurrection of Jesus. So, for a Christian who wants to move from sin to grace, from alienation to intimacy, from pain to joy, the path is to be found in virtue.

If you've read this far, you should have a clear understanding of the nature of virtue. Early Christian thinkers found themselves wrestling with the question of how a person of faith could move from a state of sin into a state of holiness through a spiritual process called sanctification. As Christians

17. Thurman, *Meditations*, 196.

moved from sin toward holiness, they discovered certain traits could nurture the process. Among these are the twelve virtues we have discussed at length, each of which has a natural component that can be understood and pursued by anyone. But true Christian virtue can be fully known only in grace, given to us by the Holy Spirit.

As presented in the introduction to this book, for St. Paul the three primary virtues were faith, hope, and love. In other places he listed many more, referring to them as the "fruit of the Spirit" or "gifts of the Spirit." Ultimately there was a kind of fluidity in this understanding. In his Letter to the Galatians, Paul listed the "fruit of the Spirit" as "love, joy, peace, patience, kindness, generosity, faithfulness, gentleness and self-control," firmly stating that "there is no law against such things" (Gal 5:22–23). In his Letter to the Colossians he focused on compassion, humility, meekness, patience, forgiveness, love, peace, thankfulness, and wisdom (Col 3:12–17). In other places he referred to discernment, knowledge, prophecy, and healing.

Those church fathers who attempted to articulate Christian virtue reached beyond the Jewish categories and sought to integrate Hellenistic ideas of the good, the true, and the beautiful. Ultimately, directed by Pope Gregory the Great, the church settled on seven virtues to echo the seven deadly sins, grafting Aristotle's four "cardinal" virtues of courage, temperance, prudence, and justice with the three "theological" virtues of faith, hope, and love. That view dominated the church's teaching for many centuries, but I find this mixture of the Hebrew and Hellenistic visions both weak and contrived. The cardinal virtues find their meaning in civic duty in classical Greek society. The Christian virtues find their meaning in the experience of salvation and sanctification that flows from a faith commitment to Jesus Christ.

Christian virtues have two unique characteristics. First, each virtue has both a natural element and a spiritual dimension. Secondly, the spiritual attribute of these virtues can only be known as a gift of grace. None of us are capable—no matter how disciplined, no matter how talented—of fully experiencing any of them on his or her own. But there is a prayer discipline which opens up a path to virtue. That discipline is described in the addendum, following another prayer discipline that presents the Circle of Forgiveness. My hope is that you, dear reader, will commit to practicing these disciplines and enter into a deeper more meaningful relationship with God.

Addendum
A Prayer Discipline for Embracing Virtue

The Human Condition

THERE IS A GOOD life. There is a way of living marked by contentment, peace, well-being, and joy. Understanding, embracing, and cultivating virtue will move us toward securing and enhancing this good life. But sin, the foundational inner attitude of human self-absorption, prevents us from enjoying it. Unless sin is addressed and dealt with, any attempt to live virtuously will be stymied time and again. Consequently, any prayer discipline designed to pursue virtue must begin with confronting and overthrowing sin. The premier way of doing that is to practice a discipline I call the Circle of Forgiveness.

The Circle of Forgiveness

Historically spiritual leaders from multiple faith traditions have found it helpful to parse the general concept of sin into its particular manifestations. In Western Christendom the seven deadly sins, codified by Pope Gregory the Great in the late sixth century, held sway until our time. They are pride, greed, gluttony, lust, envy, sloth and anger. Over the years, in trying to fathom the full scope of my own sin, I came to understand that those seven sins were simply not enough. So, I added three more: dishonesty, fear, and despair. Each of those three has both scriptural and historical precedent.

Before beginning the prayer discipline for the first time, familiarize yourself with each of the ten sins. Note the particularities of each.

- Pride is a collapse inward, a fundamental attitude of self-absorption that leads one to treat others as objects to be manipulated for personal gain. Ironically both vainglory and self-pity are manifestations of pride, because both are rooted in self-absorption. Vainglory itself can be divided into arrogance, vanity, and conceit. Those in the grip of pride have a deep need to project a false persona and blame others for our own failures.
- Greed is rooted in a basic discontent with our circumstances. No matter how much we have, we want more. It leads us to confuse needs and wants. It blinds us to the needs of others, and makes us unwilling to share what we have. It leads us to turn a blind eye to social ills like gross economic disparity, systemic racism, and environmental degradation.
- Gluttony is any compulsive or obsessive behavior that captures us, taking away our freedom. It is rooted in a lack of affirmation leading us to believe "there must be something wrong with me." In order to layer over and quell that pain and ill ease, we give ourselves over to food, or drink, or drugs, or tobacco, or sex, or possessions, or achievement. It is sin because these behaviors become our gods and enslave us.
- Lust is the desire for power, to control others. It is the opposite of vulnerability. It may result in physical and verbal abuse in families, friendships, and romance. Passive lust is manifest in the refusal to listen to others, or engage others in any meaningful way. It has a sexual component, using sex to manipulate or punish rather than for joy and heightened intimacy.
- Envy is the sin no one wants to admit. It grows out of a basic discontent with ourselves, resulting in a strange combination of self-loathing and self-love. It produces a gnawing feeling that another's success in some way diminishes us. Consequently, we are led to tear down the success of others through gossip, or we have the desire to destroy another's success through malice.
- Sloth is not laziness, but a failure to meet our primary responsibilities. We become too selfish to love in marriage, too self-centered to nurture as parents, too self-absorbed to work to become free of even our own pain.

- Anger is the sin we all know, only too well. There is appropriate anger when we are confronted with injustice or cruelty. The sin of anger is to nurture or misdirect it, taking it out on the wrong person or directing it inward, which may result in problems as diverse as depression or obesity.

- Dishonesty is elusive, as we often rationalize the comfort of a white lie rather than confront someone with plain truth. Usually, we lie to manipulate someone in order to avoid embarrassment or punishment, or to get something we want. Yet whether it be lying, stealing, cheating or fraud, dishonesty is sin not only because it harms others; it also betrays a lack of trust in God.

- Fear may be appropriate as a warning against danger. It may range from subtle anxiety to focused terror. Fear can be enslaving, cutting us off from others and preventing us from living in a godly way. It is sin because it reveals a lack of trust in God.

- Despair, called *acedia* in Western monastic tradition, is difficult to label as sin, and may perhaps be better understood as the final consequence of sin. It is essentially passive, as often those in its grip feel victimized. It can also be enslaving, shutting us off from the ability to love others. Acedia is not to be confused with depression, for at its heart it is the opposite of hope. It is the belief that when things are bad, they will never change. Thus, it is the ultimate denial of God.

Intentional confession and repentance begin with what I call the "Prayer of Stillness." Set aside an hour for each session. Settle yourself comfortably, with a pen and paper at hand (preferably a blank notebook). It will be used for journaling about your prayer experiences, so you will have a record of the insights God will be giving you. The Prayer of Stillness is an ancient prayer discipline rooted in fourth-century desert monastic traditions, designed simply to still the conscious mind. It will enable you to enter a space in your consciousness of quiet and calm, silence and peace. The same prayer has been called a variety of things, including the "prayer of silence," "contemplative prayer," and even "centering prayer." While you are in the prayer, many insights will emerge from the depths of your subconscious and unconscious mind. Just as with a dream, you will need to write them down as soon as you come out of the prayer, or you'll quickly forget them.

Choose a sacred word or phrase to begin the Prayer of Stillness. It should be a word or phrase that will foster opening yourself to God.

Historically, many Christians have used the Jesus Prayer, "Lord Jesus Christ, have mercy on me a sinner." Other appropriate phrases to use might be "Come, Lord Jesus," or "Hear me, O God," or "Have mercy on me, Lord God." Many feel it is simpler and more focused to use a sacred word, such as "grace," or "peace," or "forgiveness." William Wilson, for many years my spiritual director, uses what he calls the "Prayer of the Name," simply repeating, "Jesus, Jesus, Jesus . . ." Those who have received the gift of speaking in tongues will often intentionally pray in tongues. The key is to repeat the phrase or word with complete focus and intentionality. And bear in mind, this is very different from repeating a New Age mantra, where the meaning of the phrase is insignificant. The phrase or word you choose for this prayer must have an objective, redemptive reality. So, pick one that will open you to the Trinitarian God.

Many have found it helpful to couple the phrase or word with breath. I have used this technique in two ways. The first is to use *Yahweh*, the name of God revealed to Moses through the burning bush in Exodus 3:14. Settle yourself and with each inward breath say or think the first syllable of God's name, *Yah*, and exhaling say or think the second syllable, *Weh*. "*Yah . . . Weh. Yah . . . Weh. Yah . . . Weh.*" I have also used the Hebrew/Aramaic pronunciation of the name Jesus, which is *Yeshua*. Breath in with *Yesh*, breath out with *Hua*. "*Yesh . . . Hua. Yesh . . . Hua. Yesh . . . Hua.*"

As you become comfortable with this discipline, repeating the word or phrase, you will find your mindful attention moving into a place of quiet, stillness, and peace. Once there, you can present anything on your heart to God. For the first three days, do the prayer without any particular agenda. Once your conscious mind becomes quiet and still, simply let yourself free-associate. Flow from one thing to another, always prepared to write down what you see, what you hear, what you experience, so you won't forget anything. Trust that these free associations are being led by the Holy Spirit.

After three days of practicing the Prayer of Stillness, the next ten days will be focused on seeking forgiveness from God. You will need to set aside an hour each day to practice this discipline. You may not use the full hour, but on some days you will. Each of the ten sins will be your focus for one day. Settle yourself in a comfortable chair and read the brief description of the sin specified on that day, for example, the sin of pride. Use the sacred phrase or word to enter the place of stillness. Once in that place of quiet and calm, ask God, "Show me how I have been subject to pride." Let yourself free-associate. Give yourself over to the Holy Spirit. Let the memories flow.

A PRAYER DISCIPLINE FOR EMBRACING VIRTUE

Some will be conscious, but others will emerge from your subconscious and unconscious mind. Always be ready to write down important insights.

When you come out of the prayer, read through what you jotted in your journal on how you have been in the grip of pride. Then, again, practice the Prayer of Stillness until you find yourself in the place of deep quiet before God. Offer a particular memory of your prideful behavior to God, asking for God to forgive you and liberate you. Let yourself free-associate until you feel completion and resolution. Then offer God another memory of prideful behavior using the same practice. Bring the prayer to conclusion after you have offered seven memories to God. Be sure to write what you've experienced in your prayer journal. Then on the next day, choose another sin and follow the same protocol. Continue every day with a different sin until you have completed all ten of the sins.

After you have gone through confession and repentance of your own sins, turn your attention to the imperative that you forgive those who have harmed you. Set aside the next day, and enter the Prayer of Stillness. Hold yourself before God, asking the Holy Spirit to reveal those whom you have not forgiven. And again, some will be consciously on the surface, so come out of the prayer to jot them down in your journal. Re-enter the prayer, and let yourself free-associate, allowing the Holy Spirit to bring to mind those memories you may have repressed or forgotten. Record each in your journal. Then choose one person, re-enter the Prayer of Stillness, and hold that person before God, asking the Holy Spirit to enable you to forgive, to let go, until you feel a sense of relief. The next day you will repeat the prayer for three others on your list, once at a time. You will know that you have forgiven each when you can think of him of her and desire their well-being. Come out of the prayer after each individual in order to write in your journal. Go back into the prayer for the second and third individuals. Be prepared to use this prayer in the future, as it is likely others will cause you harm in some way.

After forgiving others, it will be time to focus on seeking the forgiveness of those whom you have harmed. Enter the Prayer of Stillness to ask God to reveal those people. Again, you may be conscious of some, but others will only emerge through free association in the prayer. Be aware that when this discipline truly takes root under the guidance of the Holy Spirit, it will reveal the full depth and power of how your sinful behavior has harmed others. Trust me, this can be startling and painful to discover. My experience has been that it's easy to gloss over the negative consequences of my behavior. I may consciously remember indents, but I've ignored just how hurtfully others have been impacted by my conduct.

Be sure to write the names and details about each circumstance in your journal. On the next day, enter the Prayer of Stillness and when you are in that place of attentive quiet, hold one instance of your harmful behavior toward others before God. Let yourself free-associate, asking God to show you what you can now do for restitution. It may not be possible to do anything. It may not be possible to contact the people you have harmed. Come out of the prayer to write down what you experienced. Repeat the process with two other situations that emerged. When it is possible and you prayerfully feel it is appropriate, at a later time get in touch with the people brought into your mind, asking for their forgiveness. Also ask them if there is anything you can do to repair the harm. This may be a task to be completed over many weeks. Keep a record of every encounter in your journal.

All three of these disciplines must be practiced to enter fully into the reality of God's forgiveness. The promise in return is that you may experience nothing short of radical inner freedom and astonishing joy. But again, the spiritual fruit is not predicated on what you experience or feel. The real promise is that you will then simply be living out the redemptive imperative of the kingdom of God. Also remember, some memories of people may have emerged during the latter two disciplines that you will need to pray about individually at a later date. Be aware, these disciplines are not done just once. You will certainly need to use them again in the future. Because you will sin again, you will be harmed again, and you will likely hurt others again, the disciplines will need to be practiced regularly. For the fullness of spiritual health and well-being, the entire three-part discipline will need to be woven into any ongoing piety.

Embracing Virtue

With the full circle of sin in your life confronted and dealt with in a redemptive way, the next step in reaching spiritual maturity is the pursuit of Christian virtue. Historically some of humanity's greatest minds have wrestled with trying to understand the nature of moral behavior and the virtues that enhance it. Virtue has been parsed philosophically, psychologically, historically, legally, and religiously. This book's deepest foundation is rooted the biblical vision of Jesus and the apostles who wrote the books in the New Testament, and builds on two thousand years of Christian theology and spirituality. The moral life, or from a Christian perspective the godly life, rests on a three-part process. There is a godly life. Sin prevents us from knowing it. Virtue is what will lead us from sin, through forgiveness, into the godly life.

There are multiple lists of virtue presented in both the Gospels and Epistles. Some teachers have feathered out over 120 virtues named in the New Testament (although many of these overlap with one another). Although I have selected only twelve, I believe they are the most important twelve for fostering spiritual maturity. All these virtues have both natural and spiritual aspects. The natural characteristics of each virtue can be known and experienced by anyone, with or without religious faith. But each of these twelve also has a spiritual quality that can only be known through the grace of God. That's why St. Paul refers to them as "spiritual gifts" (1 Cor 12:1). Unlike the natural properties of the virtues, their spiritual attributes may lead a person of faith into the presence of God.

Some of the virtues are so difficult to translate in English that I have used the words for them in the original Greek of the New Testament or the desert fathers in the fourth century. The twelve virtues are: humility, faith, hope, *agape* (unconditional love), *apatheia* (inner freedom), peace, kindness, generosity, purity of heart, *praos* (disciplined discernment), *upomone* (patient good courage), and wisdom. Before you begin the prayer discipline for the virtues, it's important to familiarize yourself with each of the twelve, so rereading specific chapters on sin has been built into the prayer discipline. The special particularities of each are detailed below:

- Humility is the opposite of pride. As pride is basic self-absorption, humility is to be selfless, not conscious of self at all. It has nothing to do with low self-esteem or self-denigration, and provides a clear sense of one's strengths as well as weaknesses. Godly humility recognizes our own inability and the necessity of relying on God. Humility leads to transparency and enables us to be a living gateway between the material and spiritual worlds.

- Faith has three distinct components. The first is assent to truth. The second is trust. The third is fidelity. Christian faith is assent to the truth of the Bible and great creeds of the church. Christian faith is to trust in God in every circumstance for our ultimate happiness, security, and welfare. Christian faith is fidelity to the will of God, not just part of the time, not just when things are going well, but all of the time, under all circumstances, to the very end of our lives.

- Hope is not optimism, which is belief in the ability to change bad circumstances. Christian hope is the sure knowledge of God's abiding love and control of history. Christian hope rests on what God has done and promises to do in the future. Christian hope destroys despair and hardness of heart. It enables us to witness for justice, and it leads to joy and peace.

- *Agape* is an utterly unconditional love seeking only the well-being of others. *Agape* accepts others as they are. *Agape* gives us the capacity to listen fully to another. It speaks the truth in love, and gives us the ability to both forgive and be forgiven. *Agape* empowers us to give up our own agenda, in the service of God and others.

- *Apatheia* is a radical inner freedom. *Apatheia* sets us free from powerful emotions and compulsions such as anger, fear, lust, envy, greed, and gluttony, which can enslave us. With *apatheia* there is no denial or repression. It enables us to feel everything but be captured by nothing. *Apatheia* was the primary virtue sought by the desert fathers of the fourth century.

- Peace is more than stillness and quiet. It is a well-being of health, contentment, and joy that fills our whole being. Unlike the world's peace, which is temporary, Christian peace lasts forever. It was the first gift the resurrected Jesus Christ gave to the apostles, and it is the gift St. Paul asked to be given to the recipients of every one of his epistles.

- Kindness is not niceness or politeness, although they may look the same on the outside. Kindness always wills the well-being of the other, and may be costly. While niceness is often self-aggrandizing, kindness seeks nothing for self. Kindness produces repentance, receivability, and transparency. It is not weak, and will speak truth to power. Gentleness is a companion of kindness.

- Generosity gives freely and unconditionally, only for the benefit of others. It is not interested in accruing any kind of reward. Generosity dethrones the power greed has in our lives, and always seeks to help those in need. Generosity enables the giver to enter into a state of thankful joy and happiness.

- Purity of heart is not about moral or theological purity, which often bleeds into intolerance. Purity of heart is to be single-minded in devotion to God. It routs out all double-mindedness, such as dishonesty, which is to know the truth but tell a lie, or hypocrisy, which is to promote one thing and do the opposite.
- *Praos* is when we offer our self-will to God and seek only God's will. It enables us to become fully human, when our whole being, our intellect and will, our emotions and imagination, are so subject to God, we will hear even God's slightest urging, and be able to freely act on it.
- *Upomone* in the New Testament is translated into English as multiple words: "patience," "endurance," "perseverance," "steadfastness," and "good courage." It is not passive or weak, but always remains in control, intelligently waiting for the appropriate moment to act. It is powerful and liberating, but also very helpful in dealing with the ordinary, when we are frustrated, bored, or depressed. It gives us freedom and peace when we desire to strike back, or when God is silent or when we are afraid.
- Wisdom is the habitual ability to make right judgments concerning life and conduct. There are two natural categories of wisdom. The first is an intuitive sense of what is good, true, and beautiful. The second is discretion, the ability to choose the best solution when there are multiple options. The third aspect of wisdom can only be known in the grace of God. It is to clearly discern God's will.

The prayer discipline designed for the pursuit of virtue also begins with the Prayer of Stillness, with which you will be familiar after having prayed through the Circle of Forgiveness. Set aside at least one hour. Settle into a comfortable chair with a pen and your prayer journal at hand. Read through the chapter in the book on the particular virtue you will be praying for. Let's say you read the chapter on humility. Once finished with the chapter, resettle yourself comfortably and use your sacred word or phrase to begin the Prayer of Stillness. Once you have entered the place of attentive quiet and peace with your consciousness, ask the Holy Spirit this question: "Show me how in my life I have experienced the virtue of humility." Let yourself free-associate, trusting your thoughts are being led by the Holy Spirit. After you have encountered a significant memory, come out of the prayer to record your insights in the prayer journal. Then again pray the Prayer of Stillness, enter the place of quiet and calm, and ask the same question. Free-associate, journal when appropriate, and continue until you have recorded at least three personal experiences of humility. Then repeat the same process on the following days with a different virtue each day until you have completed all twelve.

The day after you have worked through the last of the twelve virtues, it is time to go deeper. Choose one of the virtues. It is appropriate to use the same order as above. Settle yourself comfortably with your prayer journal at hand. Enter the Prayer of Stillness, and when you have moved into the place of peace and calm, ask God this question: "Show me, O Lord, how humility can enhance my life of faith and godliness." Let yourself free-associate, again trusting you're being led by the Holy Spirit. When you become mindful of circumstances, events, and relationships where humility will benefit you and others, come out of the prayer to record them in your journal. Then go back into the prayer until you have recorded five things in your journal. Finish the prayer by asking God a final petition: "Lord, give me humility that I might honor you." Again, give space for free association and record any insights in your journal. On the next days, offer the same prayer for each of the remaining eleven virtues. Going forward, if you weave this petition into your regular prayer disciplines, you will find yourself being mindful of your need for specific virtues when you're in particular circumstances. I have found it very helpful to seek *apatheia* when I feel anger rising within me, or to pray for humility when I feel slighted. Not only do I benefit; so do those who are freed from my acting out.

Seeking Forgiveness from God

Day 1: Practice the Prayer of Stillness without an agenda. Use a sacred phrase or word with mindfulness until you enter the place of deep quiet. Record your experiences in your prayer journal.

Day 2. Practice the Prayer of Stillness.

Day 3: Practice the Prayer of Stillness.

Day 4: Enter the stillness. Ask God, "Show me how I've been subject to *pride*." Free-associate, coming out of the prayer to record special insights in your journal. Select four memories, go back into the silence, and ask

A PRAYER DISCIPLINE FOR EMBRACING VIRTUE

God to forgive your pride. Stay in the prayer until you feel some resolution. Then go on with each of three more memories one at a time. Record all your experiences in your journal.

Day 5: Repeat the prayer with *greed*.

Day 6: Repeat the prayer with *gluttony*.

Day 7: Repeat the prayer with *lust*.

Day 8: Repeat the prayer with *envy*.

Day 9: Repeat the prayer with *sloth*.

Day 10: Repeat the prayer with *anger*.

Day 11: Repeat the prayer with *dishonesty*.

Day 12: Repeat the prayer with *fear*.

Day 13: Repeat the prayer with *despair*.

Forgiving Those Who Have Harmed You

Day 14: Enter the stillness. Ask God to reveal those you have not forgiven. Some will be conscious; others will emerge as you free-associate. Come out of the prayer to jot names in your journal. Go back into the stillness, and hold one person who harmed you before God, asking for the ability to forgive. Hold that person before God until you feel some resolution.

Day 15: Note three others who have harmed you. Enter the stillness, and offer that person as before until you feel some resolution. Repeat with the others individually. Record what you experience in your journal.

Seeking Forgiveness from Those You Have Harmed

Day 16: Enter the stillness. Ask God to show you those you have harmed. Some will be conscious; others will emerge in the free association. Write down in your journal all those who are brought to mind. Select one person. Re-enter the stillness and hold that person before God, asking if there should be restitution. After you feel some resolution, record your experience.

Day 17: Enter the stillness. Hold another you have harmed before God, praying as described above. Pray for three others in the same way. Record what you experience in your journal.

Embracing Virtue

Day 18: Enter the stillness. Select one virtue, say *humility*. Re-read the chapter on that virtue. Enter the stillness. Ask God, "Show me how in my life I have experienced the virtue of humility." Free-associate. Come out of the prayer to record what you experience. Enter the stillness again until you have recorded three instances.

Day 19: Repeat the prayer with *faith*.

Day 20: Repeat the prayer with *hope*.

Day 21: Repeat the prayer with *agape*.

Day 22: Repeat the prayer with *apatheia*.

Day 23: Repeat the prayer with *peace*.

Day 24: Repeat the prayer with *kindness*.

Day 25: Repeat the prayer with *generosity*.

Day 26: Repeat the prayer with *purity of heart*.

Day 27: Repeat the prayer with *praos*.

Day 28: Repeat the prayer with *upomone*.

Day 29: Repeat the prayer with *wisdom*.

A PRAYER DISCIPLINE FOR EMBRACING VIRTUE

Day 30: Enter the stillness. Ask God, "Show me, O Lord, how *humility* can enhance my life of faith and godliness." Free-associate. As you are mindful of circumstances, events, and relationships where humility will benefit you and others, come out of the prayer to record them in your journal. Then go back into the prayer until you have recorded five things in your journal. Finish the prayer by asking God a final petition: "Lord, give me *humility* that I might honor you." Hold that before God, and journal what you experience.

Day 31: Repeat the prayer with *faith*.

Day 32: Repeat the prayer with *hope*.

Day 33: Repeat the prayer with *agape*.

Day 34: Repeat the prayer with *apatheia*.

Day 35: Repeat the prayer with *peace*.

Day 36: Repeat the prayer with *kindness*.

Day 37: Repeat the prayer with *generosity*.

Day 38: Repeat the prayer with *purity of heart*.

Day 39: Repeat the prayer with *praos*.

Day 40: Repeat the prayer with *upomone*.

Day 41: Repeat the prayer with *wisdom*.

Day 42: Read through all the citations on virtue in your journal. Plan to include petitions for virtue in your daily life.

Bibliography

Alligheri, Dante. *Divine Comedy: Paradise*. Translated by Dorothy Sayers. New York: Penguin, 1949.
Anderson, Wes, dir. *There Will Be Blood*. Miramax, 2007.
Aristotle. *Nicomanchean Ethics*. Translated by Adam Beresford. London: Penguin, 1976.
Aquinas, Thomas. *Summa Theologica*. Claremont, CA: Coyote Canyon, 2008.
Athanasius; Gregg, Robert C., trans. *The Life of Antony and the Letter to Marcellinus*. Mahwah, NJ: Paulist, 1980.
Augustine. *Confessions*. Classic Books America, Mineola, NY: 2009.
Bainton, Roland. *Here I Stand: A Life of Martin Luther*. Nashville: Abingdon, 2013.
Beecher, Henry Ward. *The Sermons of Henry Ward Beecher*. Oxford: Legere Street, 2023.
Benedict of Nursia. *The Rule of St. Benedict*. New York: Vintage, 1998.
Bentham, Jeremy. *Introduction to the Principles of Morals and Legislation*. Dumfries & Galloway, Scotland: Anodos, 2019.
Berry, Wendell. *Jayber Crow*. Washington, DC: Counterpoint, 2000.
Book of Common Prayer. New York: Church Hymnal Corporation, 2007.
Carnegie, Andrew. *The Autobiography of Andrew Carnegie and His Essay: The Gospel of Wealth*. North Chelmsford, MA: Courier, 1920.
Cassian, John. *Conferences*. Translated by Boniface Ramsey. Mahwah, NJ: Paulist, 1997.
Chaffer, Peter. *Something Beautiful for God*. London: BBC, 1969.
Chaucer, Geoffrey. *Canterbury Tales in Modern English*. London: Penguin, 1977.
Clouzot, Henri-Georges. *The Mystery of Picasso*. 1956.
Corey, Barry H. *Love Kindness: Discover the Power of a Forgotten Christian Virtue*. Kindle ed. Carol Stream, IL: Tyndale House, 2016.
Covey, Stephen. *The Seven Habits of Highly Effective People*. New York: Simon and Shuster, 2020.
DeSales, Francis. *Introduction to the Devout Life*. Charlotte, NC: Tan, 2010.
Donne, John. *The Complete Poetry and Selected Prose of John Donne*. Edited by Charles M. Coffin. New York: Modern Library, 2001.
Emerson, Ralph Waldo. *Friendship, and Other Essays*. New York: Dodge, 1910.
Epictetus, et al. *Essential Stoic Philosophy: All in One Stoicism*. N.p.: True Power, 2017.
Evagrius Ponticus. *Praktikos*. Kalamazoo, MI: Cistercian, 1981.
Forsyth, P. T. *The Justification of God*. London: Independent, 1957

BIBLIOGRAPHY

Goffman, Erving. *The Presentation of Self in Everyday Life*. New York: Anchor, 1959.
Gregory the Great. *Moral Reflections on the Book of Job*. Athens, OH: Cistercian, 2022.
Gunther, Gerald. *Learned Hand: The Man and the Judge*. Cambridge, MA: Harvard University Press, 1998.
Hegel, G. F. W. *Introduction to the Philosophy of History*. Translated by Leo Rauch. Cambridge: Hackett, 1988.
Hobbes, Thomas. *Leviathan*. London: Penguin Classics, 2017.
Hugo, Victor. *Les Miserables*. Translated by Isabel Hapgood. N.p.: Duke Classic, 2021.
Keefe, Patrick Radden. "The Family That Built an Empire of Pain." *The New Yorker*, October 23, 2017.
Keller, Timothy. *King's Cross: The Story of the World in the Life of Jesus*. New York: Dutton, 2011.
Lao Tsu. *Tao Te Ching*. Translated by Dwight Goddard. Oviedo, Spain: Entreacacias, 2022.
Lewis, C. S. *The Great Divorce*. New York: Harper Collins, 1973.
———. *Mere Christianity*. New York: Macmillan, 1977.
———. *Surprised by Joy*. New York: Harper Collins, 1955.
———. *They Stand Together: The Letters of C.S. Lewis to Arthur Greeves, 1914–1963*. Edited by Walter Hooper. New York: Macmillan, 1976.
Machiavelli, Niccolo. *The Prince*. Translated by Harvey C. Mansfield. Chicago: University of Chicago Press, 1998.
MacIntyre, Alasdair. *After Virtue*. Notre Dame, IN: University of Notre Dame Press, 2007.
Muggeridge, Malcolm. *Vintage Muggeridge: Religion and Society*. Grand Rapids: Eerdmans, 1985.
Newman, Barbara. "Charles Williams and the Companions of the Co-inherence." *Spiritus: A Journal of Christian Spirituality* 9.1 (January 2009) 1–26.
Niebuhr, Reinhold. *The Nature and Destiny of Man*. Louisville: Westminster John Knox, 2021.
Pascal, Blaise. *Pensees*. Translated by A. J. Krailsheimer. New York: Penguin Classics, 1995.
Platinga, Cornelius. *Not the Way It's Supposed to Be: A Breviary of Sin*. Grand Rapids: Eerdmans, 1996.
Plato. *The Great Dialogues of Plato*. Translated by W. H. D. Rouse. London: Penguin Classics, 2007.
Sapolsky, Robert M. *Determined: A Science of Life without Free Will*. New York: Penguin, 2023.
Sartre, Jean-Paul. "Existentialism Is a Humanism." 1946. Translated by Philip Mairet. In *Existentialism from Dostoyevsky to Sartre*, edited by Walter Kaufman. London: Penguin, 1991.
Seneca the Elder. *Letters from a Stoic*. Translated by Robin Campbell. New York: Penguin Classics, 2021.
Shakespeare, William. *Four Tragedies*. London: Penguin, 1994.
Spinoza, Baruch. *The Philosophy of Spinoza*. Edited by Joseph Ratner and Shawn Connor. El Paso, TX: El Norte, 2010.
Stark, Rodney, and Xiahua Wang. *A Star in the East: The Rise of Christianity in China*. West Conshohocken, PA: Templeton, 2015.
Taylor, Howard. *Hudson Taylor's Spiritual Secret*. Chicago: Moody, 1932.
Taylor, Jeremy. *Selected Works*. Mahwah, NJ: Paulist, 1990.
Thurman, Howard. *Meditations of the Heart*. Boston: Beacon, 2023.
Tillich, Paul. *The Eternal Now*. New York: Scribner, 1963.

BIBLIOGRAPHY

Tokien, J. R. R. *The Hobbit and Complete Lord of the Rings.* London: Harper Collins, 1991.
Vivekananda. *Complete Works.* Calcutta: Advaita Ashrama, 1963.
Volf, Miroslav. *The End of Memory: Remembering Rightly in a Violent World.* Grand Rapids: Eerdmans, 2021.
W., Bill. *The Big Book.* New York: Alcoholics Anonymous World Services, 2002.
Ward, Benedicta. *The Desert Fathers.* New York: Penguin Classics, 2003.
Weber, Max. *The Protestant Ethic and the "Spirit" of Capitalism.* Translated by Peter Beahr, and Gordon C. Wells. New York: Penguin, 2002.
Williams, Charles. *He Came Down from Heaven.* London: Faber, 1961.
Xenophon. *The Memorable Thoughts of Socrates.* Translated by Edward Bysshe. London: Cassell, 1904.

www.ingramcontent.com/pod-product-compliance
Lightning Source LLC
Chambersburg PA
CBHW072138160426
43197CB00012B/2156